TRUE LIES

ROSS SLATER

WITH DOUGLAS WIGHT

TRUE LIES

HE FOUGHT WITH THE PARAS AND SURVIVED BOMBINGS, SHOOTINGS AND TORTURE. THEN HE DISCOVERED THE WORLD OF SINISTER UNDERCOVER OPERATIONS AS A 'SPY FOR HIRE'. THIS IS THE INCREDIBLE TRUE STORY OF THE MAN WHO INFILTRATED GREENPEACE.

JOHN BLAKE

Published by John Blake Publishing Ltd,
3 Bramber Court, 2 Bramber Road,
London W14 9PB, England

www.johnblakepublishing.co.uk

www.facebook.com/Johnblakepub facebook
twitter.com/johnblakepub twitter

First published in paperback in 2014

ISBN: 9781782194583

British Library Cataloguing-in-Publication Data:

A catalogue record for this book is available from the British Library.

Design by www.envydesign.co.uk

Printed in Great Britain by CPI Group (UK) Ltd, Croydon, CR0 4YY

1 3 5 7 9 10 8 6 4 2

All photographs from the author's collection.

All photographs from the author's collection.

Papers used by John Blake Publishing are natural, recyclable products made from wood grown in sustainable forests. The manufacturing processes conform to the environmental regulations of the country of origin.

CONTENTS

ACKNOWLEDGMENTS

Those who continue to work on the 'dark side', keep the faith. Stay lucky, stay safe.

Bob C – 22nd Special Air Service Regiment – inspired me in my early days and became a role model for my time in the army and for this I thank him. Bob's efforts helped to mould me into the soldier I became. It is a privilege to have served with you.

Rob P – also 22nd Special Air Service Regiment – sacrificed many significant things in his life just to help those suffering with combat related PTSD (post-traumatic stress disorder) with his charity Talking to Minds. Keep going, Rob: your work is vital and many good soldiers are alive today because of you.

In memory and recognition of Al Slater – 22nd Special Air

Service Regiment – killed on operations in Northern Ireland. Al was a phenomenal soldier who had the respect of many, including myself. With the hardness of steel and the heart of a lion he 'always went a little further'. As a friend you would want him but never as an enemy.

It was an honour to have served with John Geddes – 22nd Special Air Service Regiment and fellow author. Always professional, except in the NAAFI.

Corporal Paul Sullivan of 2 Para was killed in action in the Falklands War on 28 May 1982. He was not only a personal and close friend but a professional mentor who guided me through my early days in 2 Para. The bond that developed was to last for eternity and I could not have asked for a more special friend and comrade. Not only did I lose a lifelong friend but the regiment lost a brave and professional soldier who died doing what he did best.

Steve Garside – Ex-Sergeant of 2 Para and his partner Kate, I owe a great debt of gratitude for the unwavering support and kindness shown. You shouldered the burdens that many would have walked away from. I can't thank you enough and you have displayed what the airborne brotherhood really means.

It's impossible to name all those who know me and had my back in the Parachute Regiment, but a sincere thanks. When the bombs and bullets flew and the rows in the bars kicked off you were always there. A special thanks to Gordon Spence, Dave Smith (95) and Marty Magerison and, finally, to all those who have made the ultimate sacrifice – respect and *utrinque paratus*. Your duty is done: go forth to the halls of Vahalla where only the brave exist.

Bette and Alesia Sullivan (the widow and daughter of Corporal Paul Sullivan), thank you both for the many years of friendship and for keeping Paul's spirit alive. If it was not for him I would never have met two wonderful people. I sincerely thank you.

Sarah Wyatt and Toni Fry have been kind and reliable mentors over the years for which I will always be grateful for in many ways. Thank you, Sarah, from the heart.

Eddie Smyth and Tom Armstrong, thank you for the dedication, motivation and commitment to my goals, I never knew pain could be so much fun!

Martin Hall is a friend who has gone beyond what could be expected and is an exceptional guy. Good luck with P Coy.

Ross and Brett: not always easy but always easily loved no matter what.

Martin Heap is a friend, former colleague and crew partner from C Team 8 Territorial Support Group (TSG). Together we took down some of the most violent and prolific criminals in London in our time on the Group on the Green. From the south London riots and drug dealers in Soho to armed suspects in central London. Thanks for the times, Martin, and sorry about the sink – but shit happens.

Nigel Newport MBBS, DRCOG and BA is one of the most sincere and dedicated men I know. Your help and advice proved invaluable in the 25 years I have known you.

Carolyn, Elaine, Mick, Dean and Lee, I am proud and appreciative to have such a good bunch of guys around me as a family and to have a wonderful sister. Thank you.

In memory of my mother who passed away after a long, hard fight against cancer. Always inspired and supported by you to the end. Always loved. Always remembered.

Asher passed away after being my focus of comfort and companionship for so many years.

Doug Wight and Andrew Lownie had faith in me as an author and gave me the opportunity to tell my story which I know will bring much pleasure and hopefully inspiration to many people.

PROLOGUE

HEAP OF TROUBLE

Central London, 2 February 2007

Just my luck.

Two trucks on this godforsaken mission and it's the other one that breaks down. That would have been my Get Out of Jail card. A knackered truck. Nobody would ever have suspected that I had been desperate not to complete my task. In fact, as my vehicle trundled through the narrow streets of the City in London in rush-hour traffic on this bitingly cold February morning, why hadn't I thought of that? I could have rigged the engine so we didn't even leave the Farm. That would have been an idea. Although, God knows how I would have managed that with half a dozen Greenpeace people snooping around me.

Pointless thinking about it now. I was here, I was driving

and, unless I thought of something fast, I was going to be in a heap of trouble. That was almost amusing. The operation had been codenamed Project Heap, after all. We ground to a halt. The traffic was backed up. Even for a Monday morning in the capital, the place was jammed. This was turning into a cluster-fuck of massive proportions. I turned to Trevor, my co-pilot, and grimaced, shrugging at yet another hold-up. He glowered at me. This was obviously my fault.

We were 90 minutes late already for the rendezvous point. The longer we went on, the more I suspected the plan would change. Any element of surprise had long been lost. If we ploughed ahead with the original idea, we'd be stopped well before the target destination. It would be a PR disaster. That alone might even be enough for me to be burnt. It was my only hope, however. Any deviation from the script and I was fucked.

It was 8 a.m. and I was in the cab of a three-and-a-half-tonne truck. My load was a container full of coal. My destination: 10 Downing Street. At this moment, I am an activist for Greenpeace, the world's biggest and best-known environmental organisation. Today, our mission is to send a message to Prime Minister Tony Blair that the world is on the verge of a climate-change catastrophe.

The movement was furious because Blair had made coal cheaper to burn than less-polluting natural gas and had encouraged a wave of applications from energy companies to build brand-new coal-fired power stations – the first new applications in 20 years.

Greenpeace saw these power plants as the nail in the coffin for the UK's attempts to stop global warming. Our protest is timed to coincide with the publication later today of a report by the world's top climate-change experts, announcing unequivocally that global warming is a real and growing threat – and that it is definitely a man-made problem.

Greenpeace were hoping the stunt would generate headlines around the world and ruin the PM's day. What they didn't know was that Blair knew they were coming. And so did Special Branch. A team of cops would most likely be there waiting to arrest them. How did I know this? Because I tipped them off. You see, what Greenpeace also didn't know was that I am a double agent. I worked for Greenpeace, giving them the benefit of my expertise on security issues – gleaned from 30 years experience with the army and the police.

But I am also a covert source for Special Branch (SB), alongside UK PLC, who are MI5 and MI6; they are effectively the government's police force. For the last five years, I have been keeping my Special Branch handlers informed of everything Greenpeace was up to, either in the UK, or internationally.

You might wonder why the government or the police would care what a bunch of tree-huggers, as the force likes to term them, were getting up to. In the age of globalisation, many protest groups know that the only way to get their message heard is to strike at the heart of government and big business. Previously, so-called peaceful demos in London had resulted in widespread disruption, costing the taxpayers millions of pounds. And, just two years earlier, when Islamic terrorists had brought the capital to a standstill with a series of suicide bombs, they had struck in the wake of mass demos to mark the G8 summit held at Gleneagles in Scotland.

No one likes surprises, least of all police forces fighting a renewed terror or protest threat, or governments fighting to restore order in an age of unrest.

Keep your enemies close – it's a saying going back to the dawn of time. First quoted by Chinese military general Sun Tzu in his treatise *The Art of War,* it's as relevant today as it was then.

For years, SB didn't have a clue what was going on in the minds of environmentalists – until I showed up. Since I hooked up with Greenpeace, I've been taken hostage, caught plotting a protest at a nuclear power station and nearly arrested outside Number 10. But I've also given SB prior warning on all stunts and protests and recently provided them with the most comprehensive dossier on the organisation's global hierarchy that law enforcement has ever received.

Now, here I was, on the frontline once again. If all things went to plan, we'd dump our coal outside Blair's gaff. I'd be fine because I've been granted immunity from prosecution. But if something goes wrong – if there's a change of plan – then I was screwed. My immunity only extended to Downing Street. If Greenpeace chiefs decided on another target, I wasn't protected.

And since we'd left Greenpeace's secret holding base (well, secret until I blew the lid on it) at 4 a.m. this morning, things had been massively going wrong.

The plan was for two trucks – seven tonnes of coal. We'd lost one on the way. Now it was just me. A succession of events had made me think for the first time in five years that Greenpeace were on to me. I now had a companion alongside me in the cab in a position to watch my every move.

At 8.30 a.m., we crawled over the Thames and finally made our rendezvous point in Upper Ground, on the South Bank, near the ITV studios. There, a dozen activists dressed in bright-orange boiler suits stripped the lorry of its covers, revealing huge GREENPEACE – BLAIR DUMPS CLIMATE banners on the side.

We needed to get a move on. Any later and it wouldn't be worth doing. We had to be at Number 10 before the PM left for his first appointment.

Just then, Kevin, the middleman between me and our action-unit coordinator who was on foot patrol checking the situation in Whitehall, approached me. He looked stressed.

'There's been a change of plan,' he said.

'What the fuck do you mean?' I said.

'There are too many cops on Westminster Bridge. The place is crawling with them. It's like they know we're coming.'

Fuck, I thought. What the hell were the Met playing at? First, they'd declined my request to have my protection extended to include other potential targets nearby, then they'd promised to have only their usual levels of policing on show. No funny business, I had said.

I couldn't understand it. Were they finally burning me? Had I outlived my usefulness? After all this time, after everything I'd done – and how pleased they'd seemed with my work– was this it?

'So what's the plan now?' I asked Kevin.

'Change of plan,' he said. 'We're hitting DEFRA.'

I fucking knew it. DEFRA was the Department of Environment, Food and Rural Affairs. It was half a mile away from Downing Street and a viable alternative target.

'Whatever happens, don't get arrested,' my SB handler had told me.

'You need to move,' Kevin shouted. 'Get to DEFRA now!'

This is it, I thought. I'm toast.

CHAPTER 1

PUTTING YOUR LIFE ON THE LINE

You don't wake up one morning and think: 'I'm going to be a double agent.'

To get to where I ended up with Greenpeace, I travelled a long and arduous path. The truth was I didn't have a clue what I wanted to be when I was growing up. Born and raised in Lambeth, South London, as the son of a bus driver, I was never that fond of school and the thought of working hard to learn a profession was never on the agenda.

I'm sure there were times my parents despaired that I would never make anything of myself. I was content to muck around with my mates and, although I wasn't a bad child, I did have my moments. My parents divorced and I ended up living with my mum and sister in a flat in Stockwell. I was desperate to find a way out of my mundane existence and knew that, for a while, that escape route might lead nowhere but prison.

I had mates who graduated from youthful pranks to petty crime. One chum in particular went from small-time stealing to armed robbery and ended up spending time at Her Majesty's pleasure while the rest of us were at home watching *Crackerjack*.

In September 1974, at the ripe old age of 16, I left my school in Brixton with average exam results and sat down to contemplate long and hard about what the hell I would do with my life. I thought about the police because some of the family had worked for them in a civilian role but, although it was appealing, I just imagined that there was more to life than smacking yobs round the ear for nicking apples.

No, what interested me was a career with more action and a chance to see the world. I had a fantasy, somewhat skewed as it would turn out, that the military would provide a life of sun, sea, bullets, bars and birds. I figured the army was the place for me. My father had been in the navy but, whenever I broached the subject with him of joining the armed forces, his response was always the same: 'Why would you want to do that?'

He hadn't enjoyed his time in the military and he had perfectly reasonable concerns about Northern Ireland, which in the 1970s was a hotbed of violence.

Interestingly, my mother did not rule it out, so I began to realise that she might be the weak link if I was to break down their resistance.

In the short term, however, I agreed with their requests to find a job in civvy street, so one morning I went down to a local factory where apprenticeships were going for fitters. To my horror, I was offered one. I felt duty bound to accept it and returned home to tell my mum the good news. I was to start in two weeks time but, in that intervening period, that yearning to give the army a crack never left me.

A day after I received the paperwork to start my new position, I couldn't resist any longer and made my way over to Battersea Bridge Road and the army recruiting office. I hesitated outside and hovered nervously, looking into the window displays that illustrated a life full of fun and adventure in the most exotic locations in the world. I took a deep breath and pushed open the door to the office and took my first steps into another world.

I filled in some paperwork and completed a few tests and, as I waited for the results from the recruiting sergeant, I noticed on the furthest table a glossy picture of a paratrooper wearing a red beret, and in the background another photograph of a plane surrounded by hundreds of parachutes in the sky. Curiosity got the better of me, and I leaned over and picked up the photo. Again, in a daze and unaware of my surroundings, I fumbled through the photos, the silence broken by the sharp bark of Ginge – the sergeant – catching me swooning over the photos.

'That's a hard one, it's tough, and it's not easy to get into,' he said.

'Tell me more,' I said.

Even though he did his best to dissuade me and explained that the failure rate of selection to the Paras was almost 75 per cent, my mind was made up. I wanted to be a paratrooper. He asked me to think about it for a couple of weeks and said that, before anything could happen, he would want to come round and speak to my mother.

I turned up for my first day at the factory with a heavy heart but went through the motions and completed my induction day. On leaving, however, I had what could either be described as a moment of clarity or a rush of blood to the head. I strode into the personnel office and announced my plans to quit for the army.

'And what will you do if your career in the army doesn't work out?' the personnel manager said.

'Well, I guess I'll come back here then,' I said.

I went home and told my mum my decision and that I'd asked the army to send a representative round to speak about a possible career. Mum reluctantly agreed, but my dad was adamant: he would refuse to sign my enlistment papers. As it turned out, I didn't need my dad's permission. After my mum spoke at length to Ginge, she signed on the dotted line and my dreams suddenly became a reality.

Before long, I was shipped off to Aldershot to begin my training. What a rude awakening that was to be. We marched, we ran, we carried heavy weights everywhere and received what I felt was a life-threatening initiation to the Paras. I soon learnt that the regiment had a reputation for fighting, drinking and shagging and were feared among even the hardest of men. Over 60 per cent of the SAS are former Paras, a figure that says it all about the regiment. Within a few months, I had lost so much weight that even I did not recognise myself, but I felt better for it and already had made a lot of friends from all over the United Kingdom. The training was relentless – day and night – and your bed was often no more than an unobtainable dream. I had arrived in Aldershot a boy and in little more than four months had been transformed into a man.

Soon it was my turn to leave the junior regiment and take on the recruit platoon training, which was where you were either made or broken. In my recruit platoon, 38 started the six months and only 17 passed as fully-fledged qualified paratroopers. Over the next few months, I was to experience pain like I'd never thought possible before. The arrogant attitude I had back in South London soon disappeared, but my inner strength grew and, with it, a quiet air of confidence and maturity.

On reflection, many people say that ex-Paras lose their fitness after leaving the regiment, which is true in some cases, but the one thing that does stick is the ability to remain mentally strong and determined beyond most civilian capabilities, something that becomes invaluable on covert operations.

After many months of sheer hard work and personal development came P Company week, which is designed to test the recruit in all disciplines relative to his role. This will determine if he makes the regiment or is transferred to a less demanding role within another unit, or in some cases receives a complete discharge from the army. Endless mental pressure to succeed, coupled with raw physical ability, is applied in various scenarios, including the Trainasium (an assault course set 60 feet above ground, designed to test the ability to overcome fear and to follow simple orders at considerable height), steeple chase, log race, milling, ten-mile speed tab, assault course, and other such delights designed to exert maximum pressure on the recruit.

The parachute-jump course was the penultimate test before the end of basic training. When I had completed seven jumps and was on my last before earning my wings, an accident occurred. A bad exit from the aircraft at night left me with severe twists in my parachute rigging lines. I had failed to take into account my height and hit the ground still kicking out of my twists; I went in like a corkscrew, and broke an ankle. After a few months in plaster, I returned, gained my wings, and earned the title of an airborne soldier. By now, all of my dreams had come true and confirmed – when I passed out from training.

All my dreams as a youth were now a reality. At last, I was where I wanted to be.

I was posted to 2 Para and it wasn't long before I had my first tour of duty to Northern Ireland. At that time, we were the Spearhead battalion, better known as the 24-hour response unit for any trouble that occurred anywhere in the world, so all our kit was already packed and ready to go. Periods of FIBUA (fighting in built-up areas) training took place along with range work. The time came and we were sent on pre-deployment leave. I went home and had my blood group tattooed on my right forearm (I don't know what I would have done if I'd lost that arm in an explosion).

Arriving in Belfast, we were amazed to see that our base was located smack between the Falls Road and the Shankhill Road – in other words, the Catholics at one end of the street and the Protestants at the other! On that first tour of duty, I made a lot of what would become lifetime friendships, none closer than Paul Sullivan.

Northern Ireland was an extremely challenging environment and in many ways a baptism of fire to life in the armed forces. On an attachment with the Royal Military Police, we were ambushed and came under heavy fire.

I then faced the agonising decision of whether to take action against a woman with a pot of burning-hot fat, who was threatening to douse me and a cordon of soldiers with it. After repeatedly warning her to stay back, I had no option but to halt her progress. I did so by firing a baton round into the ground in front of her. It ricocheted upwards and hit her in her midriff, sending her backwards onto a car, the pot falling harmlessly away. It was a split-second decision but one that I would make again in similar circumstances and I was praised for my actions.

Just as I neared the end of that first tour, I was caught in the type of incident no soldier wants to go through. I was on a patrol in North Howard Street, near Falls Road, when the world stood still, everything then moved in slow motion. The sounds around me faded to silence and then I was aware of debris falling on top of me and I was bleeding.

The wreck of a nearby Volkswagen Beetle told me we had been the victims of a car bomb – the first-ever remote-controlled device used in the province. The blood was the result of flying VW car bits. I was never so glad to see a car go out of production as the VW Beetle. Incredibly, no one was killed but it was a warning how real the threat from the IRA was on a daily basis.

Overseas postings followed on from there, including a bizarre stint at Brooke Barracks, Spandau, where we played our part in the protection of Nazi war criminal Rudolf Hess.

In the times I saw Hess wandering around the garden, I often thought of him as the loneliest man on earth. He had no visitors, no papers, no TV news. I was directed to never ever make contact with him, give him anything, or pay any sort of attention to the man, as a British soldier on duty had previously given Hess sweets and cigarettes. But on one particular occasion, I was in one of the watchtowers when

Hess walked up to the bottom as if he was coming up the stairs. He stopped short and slowly raised his head and stared at me. His eyes were ice cold, with no apparent emotion; it was obvious his mind was as cold as any winter, and he remained fixed on me for some minutes, which was eerie by any standards. He then broke the stare and slowly turned away from me, glanced down, and walked slowly away. That was the last time I saw Hess alive. It was an extraordinary experience. The feeling still haunts me to this day, and I still ponder over what he was thinking of me that time. I'll never know.

Around the beginning of 1979, we had a visit from the SAS, who were in Berlin to see the regiment on a recruitment drive. At this time, I was only a few months from either signing off or staying on. If I were to stay on, I would try selection. After thinking long and hard and seeing my civilian counterparts, I decided I would try life outside of the 'big family'. If things didn't work out, I had an option to rejoin the regiment and return straight to where I had come from.

I decided I wanted a fresh challenge and, therefore, applied and was accepted to Thames Valley Police. A new life beckoned. I knuckled down to police training and settled into my new role but, at the moment when it became impossible to resurrect my army career – had I wanted to – I found I was yearning for that camaraderie that only a regiment could give you. With my opportunity to return to the army now gone, I had to find an alternative to supplement my growing disappointment with civvy street. After a few enquires and telephone calls, I presented myself one evening at the squadron offices of 21 Special Air Service

Regiment, Territorial Army Volunteer Reserve, and signed up for service. Volunteering with the Territorial Army (TA) gave me a new lease of life and made my service in the police a little more tolerable.

The weekends were hard, intense and challenging, but this was what I had missed and, over time, I began to find myself dedicated more to the TA than the police.

I was assigned to a drugs unit and posted as station officer but, in 1982, my world collapsed. I got the word that my old buddy from the Paras, Paul Sullivan, had been killed in action in the Falklands. After the initial tidal wave of shock overwhelmed me, it was explained to me that Paul had been at Goose Green and had gone forward with his platoon commander and others to take an implied surrender from a heavily fortified Argentinian position. Something had gone wrong and the enemy position opened up with terrifying firepower on those who had gone forward and slaughtered the group at one fell swoop, killing them all instantly. Paul was killed and had suffered multiple gunshot wounds to his head and body. He would have felt no pain, so the story goes.

Paul was the best friend I had ever had and we had practically grown up together. He left behind his wife, Shirley, who had not long before given birth to their daughter, Alesia.

His funeral was one of the saddest days of my life – a time not to say goodbye but to ask him to keep my place in the drop zone in the sky. If it is possible for one man to love another, this was it.

Before the ceremony, I stood in the regimental gym beside Paul's coffin, which was draped in a Union Jack, his beret and bayonet neatly placed on top. Other mates' coffins were lined up in regimental fashion in perfect ranks and included Steve Prior and Gaz Bingly, two other close friends. As they were laid to rest in the military cemetery, the guard of honour fired their salute, and sounding of the 'Last Post' silenced any background noise. As I stood over the grave, a solitary teardrop fell from my eyes and seemed to take an age to reach the coffin below. When it did, it hit the brass nameplate, the delivery of an unmistakable kiss to a lost friend.

Life was almost suspended for me during this time, and the only thing that kept me going was the time away with the TA regiment.

Even now, you will find me sitting next to the grave, in the quiet of the wonderful cemetery, and talking over the times we had together. Only the trees talk of the heroes that lie beneath their roots. I, too, will be going there in future times, my place booked to return home to be with my friends when it is my time to leave this crazy and fucked-up world.

I threw myself into my police career and earned the nickname 'Golden Bollocks' because of my high arrest rate. Yet, despite my exemplary record, I was astonished when, one day, four years into my service, I was summoned to see the superintendent. He raised the issue of my involvement with the TA and said it wasn't compatible with a police career. If I wanted to continue in the force, I would have to give it up. It was an easy decision to make. After years pounding the streets, I was once again faced with the reality of a career change.

Given the skills I'd acquired in the army and the police,

I decided to become a consultant in the security world. I completed a close-protection course with a company run by some ex-SAS lads and that led to a plum gig working at the London residence of the Sultan of Brunei. For the first time in years, I enjoyed my work. It was also the time I met and married my wife, Carol. For the time being at least, I felt settled.

My role with the sultan was fairly straightforward but, one day, I was off-duty when I got a call from one of the lads at the residence. A theft had taken place in the princess's room and jewellery worth millions of pounds had been stolen. An insurance claim went in and, although no one was ever found responsible for the theft, the security team were above reproach because none of us had access to the room. The most startling thing about the incident, however, was that the attitude to the loss was about the same as if someone had lost a sock. That was as excited as the royal household got about it.

Unfortunately, after about a year, a staff turnaround meant I was looking for another assignment. Although I picked up work on a piecemeal basis, I was looking for something to get my teeth into. Ideally, I wanted to try my hand at covert work. I realised my best chance of getting into the under-cover business was to join the specialists – the Met.

In 1990, I began my training at Hendon Police College and my career with the Metropolitan Police started with a posting to Dagenham and Barking. After eight months finding my feet again as a police constable (PC), I applied to the central Territorial Support Group (TSG) at Paddington Green. The TSG was renowned for its proactive policing methods and this was frontline policing at its finest. My personal arrest rate soon rocketed past the 400 mark.

Still desperate to sample some covert work, I applied for a surveillance course, which ultimately led to a posting with the Flying Squad. That only served to whet my appetite, but I was due to return to the TSG shortly. It was then that I ended up in hospital with a smashed collarbone, after my vehicle was rammed by a stolen car that earlier had hit a PC.

With the Met, you never know what's lurking around the corner – particularly so in the 1990s when the threat of an IRA attack was still very much a constant danger. So it proved when, on one Saturday morning at around 8 a.m., I was preparing to go running near Paddington Green Police Station. I was walking to the security point by the rear entrance of the station when suddenly I was hit by a blast wave that sent me flying on to my backside. I lay there stunned, being showered with debris. I was completely deaf and disorientated. It took me a few moments to realise what had happened: I had been caught in another bomb blast.

I got the same taste back in my mouth as I'd had that day in North Howard Street, when our patrol had been bumped. As I looked around, I could see nothing except glass falling from the upper-level canteen of the nick. I knew I should stay put, in case of a secondary device, but, some-how, I needed to see if there were casualties. I managed to get to my feet and move to the opposite side of the road, diagonally, to open up my view of the front of the nick. My ears were ringing and I was sweating badly. I felt weak from the waist down. As I glanced around the corner, I couldn't see the telephone kiosk that had been there a few minutes earlier. Now it was just wires pointing up from the ground, and a load of buckled and twisted metal and glass.

Yet again, I had escaped death through sheer luck. The IRA had planted a bomb packed in a plastic sandwich box in the telephone kiosk.

Not as a response to that incident, but due to an illness in my family, my service on the TSG was, unfortunately, cut short, as I took a posting to a station outside London to be nearer home. In the years that had followed our marriage, Carol and I had been blessed with three children, Harriet, Jacob and Clare.

I was still in uniform for the time being and my dreams of undercover work had to be put on hold for now.

Once my family situation had calmed down, I was itching for some action and applied to join Stoke Newington station. Within a week, I had transferred and was soon up to my neck in stabbings, murders, drugs and fatal accidents. My arrest count was now up to nearly 850, and I earned seven commendations and a Royal Humane Society award.

As my career progressed, I managed to join the proactive team, which brought into play my surveillance skills and covert camera skills. On one operation in Dalston, in Hackney, I was tasked with gathering evidence on an overseas-telephone-call company that was a front for dealing drugs. The observation point selected was the best of a bad situation, so someone was needed to take a covert position directly opposite the shop itself. Of course, I offered to do it. It was what I wanted most of all. I arrived on duty in old, worn-out trainers with old trackie bottoms and a huge, oversized overcoat tied up with string in the middle. My face had not seen a razor in days and I had a lone piece of string, which was missing that all-so-standard vagrant dog! Through luck, in the police station, we had a tramp and his dog, and both stank to hell in the rain. We borrowed the tramp's dog.

Accompanied by a full covert surveillance team, including photographers and spotters, I went off in the pouring rain to position myself outside a bank on the pretext that I was hoping for some handouts from people using the cash machine. The team were in offices above the bank.

One well-heeled punter even chastised me for scrounging off the state and said I should join the army instead. By this time, I wanted to just place him firmly on his arse and stick my warrant card a centimetre in front of his nose, but, no, I had to swallow it or blow the op. He must have stood there for ten minutes, lecturing me about how bad I was. Eventually, he began to walk off, but not before spitting on my left shoulder. Another few hours went by, and the flow of the punters was building up inside the call company. The big boss arrived, the one we knew was the main backer, together with a big black male as his minder. A lot of exchanges took place between bags and cash – a drug drop had been made – and the boss was loading up a large black satchel and handing it to the minder.

By now, the arrest teams were on full standby to follow the two subjects and make arrests away from the immediate area. Just as I was waiting to give my command for the signal for the second phase, a very polite young lady approached, asking if I was all right. She said, 'It seems to me that you deserve a meeting with the Lord to find your lost way in your life. You are one of his children.'

Well, I'd survived the Paras, two bombs and the Met. How

lucky was that? I felt I was doing OK without any divine intervention. Unless of course, my lucky escapes meant I was indeed one of God's children already!

I gave the signal to move the raid and within seconds the immediate area was flooded with dogs and search teams. My job was over, so I bundled up my worldly goods under my arm – not forgetting the £7.51 I had collected.

The experience only served to remind me how much I wanted to be doing this type of work and so, when notice came out from Scotland Yard asking for officers to submit reports of interest in becoming undercover officers with SO10 – now the Met's Covert Operations Group – I jumped at it. I worked tirelessly, collating and structuring my application form to include all salient parts and supporting evidence, leaving no stone unturned, to provide a persuasive and eye-catching account that would earn me a place where I wanted to be.

The day came when the application was complete and so I handed it to my line manager to endorse and comment upon. Fortunately, it had gone through my uniform sergeants and inspectors, leaving little room for contradiction by the CID supervisors who would get this once all the recommendations had been placed on the supporting-comments section. Damage limitation was basically the name of the game now.

The following week proved to be a nerve-racking one, and I was forever checking my paperwork tray for any news of my application. Time between this was spent studying case law relative to undercover operations and stings that had made the news for one reason or another, plus the very grey area of agent provocateur and associated subjects. Another potential area of contention was what exactly police officers in an undercover role were allowed to do with authority. Well, the answer to this was easy. Look at what they cannot do, was the advice given to me by a mate who had worked undercover already and who later went on to be recruited by MI5.

On the ninth day after my application had been submitted, I was called in to see the Detective Chief Inspector (DCI). She said, in her opinion, I was too old for undercover operations. I was 36 at the time.

I was devastated. It smacked of discrimination, as I knew undercover officers who were older than I was. I took it up with my superiors and at one stage it looked as if the Police Federation might get involved, but, eventually, I was simply advised to apply again when next the call went out.

Force orders came out one summer and invited applications for officers to transfer to the Specialist Operations Group 16, Diplomatic Protection Group (DPG). By then, my morale was at a low, I was treading water and, although the DPG was not renowned for being proactive and had a reputation of being the department that coppers who couldn't copper went to, I decided to apply. Some senior colleagues advised me not to, saying it would not do my chances of becoming an undercover officer any good. However, I decided it would give me an even greater skill base and a chance to look at things in slow time. I started at DPG HQ, at Apex house, in Charing Cross, and completed the basic protection course that would take me well above the civvy-street standards for diplomatic security. I didn't know if that was where I was heading but, having grown disillusioned with the police, it was a realistic possibility.

My assignments included accompanying the Turkish ambassador on his duties but, when an opportunity came to join the protection team for the former Chilean dictator General Augusto Pinochet, I put my name forward. He was being held under house arrest in Wentworth in Surrey. The first day, I turned up in smart casuals, went to the armoury and got my personal weapon and ammunition allowance for the job. Now this was beginning to make me feel a lot happier and I saw it as a good move in support of my life's aim.

Our duty was a three-point operation, in that we would either be on perimeter defence, on downtime or escorting the general himself around the gardens and to hospital if needed. The general was a person I couldn't work out at first, although apart from the normal pleasantries, I was advised not to engage in conversation with him, a bit like the scenario with Rudolf Hess in Berlin. But, at times, he would just walk around the huge expanse of gardens to the rear of the property and look a beaten man. Sometimes he would have visitors, like his family; and former Prime Minister Margaret Thatcher, who was a keen friend and supporter, often visited him. When she arrived, I would be standing in the background with my ears switched off to the conversations.

Being the diplomatic group, you might expect them to be a positive force for relations with other countries but one cock-up nearly caused an international incident. Fortunately, I was on leave when delegations from Israel and Lebanon were in London for talks. It is protocol to ensure the security of either nation, and this included accommodation at the hotel. The DPG was responsible for planning and had a token presence. Unfortunately, the Israelis ended up on the same floor as the delegation from Lebanon. The bodyguards from both countries stood there glaring at each other, and Gunfight at the O.K. Corral seemed imminent, since the officers were allowed firearms in the United Kingdom. Someone from ops planning was seriously in the shit over this, and it could have easily led to a breakdown in talks between the two countries, let alone the potential for a public dispute had it all kicked off on the landing. Thankfully, it simmered down when peace was restored and one delegation agreed to move.

In October 2000, after ten years with the Met, I decided to hand in my notice. I had the offer of a job in Cairo, as a chief instructor at a military base in Nasr City. Although my time with the DPG had delivered all that I'd hoped it would, my overall impression of the Met was that it was driven by personalities and, if your face didn't fit, you were never going to get on. I wanted to improve and test myself and saw this overseas posting as a fresh challenge.

It was to be a short-term project, so I left Carol and the children at home and moved to Cairo on my own. I was going to be living in the barracks, a throwback to my time in the Paras. Life in Egypt was surprisingly easy to adjust to – a complete contrast to what I had been used to back in the Big Smoke. The days were taken up with planning courses in firearms and anti-kidnap scenarios and I was delighted to be involved in projects that were attuned to my personal goals. My boss's brother was a senior officer in the Egyptian Secret Police, which happened to be based next door to the barracks I was living in. I began to learn a lot from the special unit, especially concerning counterterrorism techniques.

As chief instructor, I was given the holding rank of captain, which was not as special as it sounds and just afforded me a few privileges. Once I had established my training programme, my job was done and it was back to the United Kingdom and off to find my next assignment, in Britain or abroad.

I desperately wanted to try my hand at some covert work. Luckily, I didn't have to wait for an assignment – one that, while decidedly unglamorous, would put me firmly on the path to becoming an undercover agent.

CHAPTER 2

THE SPY WHO WENT INTO THE COLD

GOD, it was cold.

Even with the adrenalin pumping, I could still feel the chill through to my bones.

Frost was already starting to form on the windscreen of the beaten-up old BT van and I had to yank the door open. I looked skywards before climbing in. The blanket of stars signalled that temperatures would drop even further. The van seat was a slab of ice and my breath misted the windscreen.

Bloody rust bucket. It would be just my luck if the blasted thing didn't start tonight. After a painful wheeze and splutter that made my heart miss a beat, the engine limped into life. I waited for it to catch and turned the heater on. The motor whirred convincingly but the cool waft that emerged from the vent had as much effect on the glistening window as a kitten's breath. I had to wipe it clear with my sleeve.

It was time to get going. Any sign of holding back might look suss.

The set-up was the same as previous nights but this time the bounty even more lucrative. The van had already been loaded with frozen lamb. It would certainly stay chilled in this cold. The boxes of it could net me a tidy profit if sold on the black market.

In my mirrors I could see the rest of the crew getting ready to set off at the end of the shift, their cars and vans also loaded to the brim with that night's loot – choice cuts stolen from the company larder.

I waved acknowledgment of a job well done to Brian and Steve who passed me in their transit, tooting in response to my thumbs-up.

Everything was going according to plan. I'd done my bit. The only question was whether the cops would do theirs. Nearly four months it had taken to get to this moment. Please, don't let it screw up now.

It was now January 2002 and it had been two years since I'd left the Met. Since I'd come back from Cairo, I had stumbled upon Countrywide Investigation Services (CIS), a private security firm that was staffed exclusively by ex-Flying Squad. These guys were a living, breathing homage to *The Sweeney*. They were headed by Trevor Biggs, a 45-year-old former detective. Immaculately dressed, with hardly a hair out of place, he had his team of five ex-cops well drilled, but there was a camaraderie missing from some modern cop shops. At the end of a busy week, their hard-earned pay packets were invested in the local boozer. It was a welcome environment to come into.

Back in Biggs's office, before all this started, it had seemed straightforward enough. The Sarge – everyone still called him that even though he'd been out of the Flying Squad for years – was his usual abrupt self when he'd called me in that crisp October morning.

'Fucking pricks think they're so clever,' he said, in his usual charitable manner.

He explained the scam. The late shift at a remote frozen-foods wholesaler was skimming stock from the firm. Not just the leftovers or end-of-line, mind you. The A-grade-quality stuff. Everyone was involved, including the shift manager.

It had been going on for months.

'Amazing they got away with it so long,' I remarked.

'They haven't. The bean counters spotted the discrepancies ages ago. It just took time to work out a pattern.'

I looked at him quizzically.

'This is where you come in.'

The company wanted someone to go undercover and infiltrate the gang knocking off the stock and compile enough evidence to secure some convictions. That someone was me.

My senses tingled at the anticipation of a proper job.

'I'm all ears,' I said.

By then I'd been working with the CIS boys for five months but already I had shown enough to be a trusted fixture. It was good to feel valued again.

Biggs explained the frozen-food-firm job would be a long-term undercover op. I'd be going in as a general hand in the cold-store warehouse, working the back shift when all the stock was vanishing. My cover story was that I was fresh out of the army and, with bills to pay, needed any kind of manual work to make the adjustment to civvy street. It was a situation I didn't have to lie that much about.

The only tools I was given to assist me in the operation were a beaten-up old yellow BT van and a tape recorder I was to plant in the shift manager's office.

The op was to be supervised by the regional crime squad but the only person within the firm who would know of my existence was the finance director who'd uncovered the scam.

Two days later, I prepared for my first shift as a general store hand at Finefreeze. My uniform? A scruffy T-shirt, tatty jeans, an old black bobble hat, an earring and two days stubble.

The warehouse was in the middle of nowhere, at the end of a dirt track near Bishop's Stortford in darkest Hertfordshire. It was predetermined that I would be working the late shift – 2 p.m. until 10 p.m. – the rota when all the thieving was apparently going on.

Shortly before 2 p.m., I was standing in the yard, looking like a social outcast, and my breath rank from the fags I'd smoked while I waited for the shift manager to come down.

Eventually, he appeared and introduced himself as Steve Burton. He looked in his late 30s but dressed as though he was ten years younger. Despite his relatively lowly status in a successful, yet middling firm, I detected an over-inflated sense of his own importance. He seemed cocksure and brash and, while it might have been premature to judge him without the necessary evidence, I was confident he was up to his neck in the scam.

After a tour of the warehouse and a nodding introduction to some of the 14 colleagues who shared my shift, we chatted for a while. One thing I'd learned in this line of work was that it was vital to have a legend, a cover story. The best ones should have an element of truth, so you can talk around the subject with confidence, and the story must be able to stand up to scrutiny by the targets.

After my chat with Steve, I felt I'd convinced him well of my plausible back-story. But when he led me into the canteen to meet the rest of my shift, I realised he must have been relieved I knew how to breathe and tie my own shoelaces. What a lot of misfits this lot were.

Quickly, I assessed the situation. The shift was made up of 14 people who had to process frozen-food supplies for the wholesaler and load them to trucks for clients, including some of the country's leading supermarket chains. It was a fairly basic set-up. The solitary warehouse, at the end of a remote dirt track, was approximately 120 feet wide and 60 feet high, with three loading bays.

My job involved keeping the cold store clean and tidy. This was more arduous than it sounds – given it was minus 20 – and the sweeping out took a lot of time as the floor was constantly slippery with bits of packaging and food. I felt like an icicle by the end of my first shift.

Other duties included having to climb the 20-feet racking to make sure the pallets put there by the forklift were safe and not going to fall or break up. The work was low-skill, repetitive and dull. No wonder these guys were looking to make it more interesting.

Without setting myself any unrealistic targets, I used the first days and weeks as a settling-in period while I sussed out the shift workers and tried to establish the pattern for swiping stock.

In the early days, more often than not, I was sent home before my shift ended. The excuse was often that the work was done for the day or that one of my colleagues would finish up for me, but I suspected that they were keen to get rid of the new guy so they could get on with nicking the gear.

On other occasions, I'd be sent on the fish-and-chip run for the shift and again I figured they'd be using the time to load up the stock to be stolen.

When you've spent time in the army – not a place for shrinking violets – you learn to get by being able to strike up conversation with anyone and that experience proved invaluable in making chat with these misfits. I regaled them with tales from the Paras and bent their ears with moans about how tough life was out of the service.

After I'd been there for about six weeks, the foreman, Brian, asked if I fancied a card school and a few beers after work with some of the lads. It was to be a welcome drink so they could get to know me a bit better.

At last, I thought, a chance to gain their confidence. Could this be an opportunity for a piece of the action?

He didn't have to ask twice.

When the shift ended, I joined six of the gang back at Brian's house. He lived nearby on a council estate and it seemed most of the lads were local too.

The card school was an infrequent event but when it was on it was arranged with near-military precision, with players only being notified on the day and its existence only revealed to a select few.

When we got to Brian's house, he led us through the back of the house to a spare bedroom that had been set aside for our use. Whenever I go into any situation I always like to scope the place out and assess any danger points and my escape route. It didn't take long to assess this place.

A table and chairs were already set up with glasses and ashtrays, and a stack of beer and spirits lay in the corner. There were nibbles and snacks on a small square picnic table next to the alcohol stack. In any situation, if possible, I always make a point of sitting next to a window and facing the door, to identify the first signs of trouble and so I can get the hell out of there if need be. It was a technique I first learned in the army but it served me well out of the service.

I paid my £20 fee to be in the game and, within moments, we were lost in the private smoke-filled den – with the only evidence of other people in the house being the occasional sound of children laughing and screaming in some other room.

I was a little older than the rest – most were in their mid-20s – and as one they seemed to harbour little career prospects and saw their work as little more than something to pass the time. As the game wore on, and the drink flowed, I hoped tongues would be loosened and they'd let me into their little scam but on that first night no one was forthcoming. The festivities ended about 1 a.m. but, as everyone spilled onto the street before some staggered home, I felt a barrier had come down.

The change happened even sooner than I expected. The following night, I stayed to the end of my shift and all became clear.

I was sweeping out the cold store when three men came in and started dismantling pallets of frozen food. They had what amounted to be a shopping list and divvied up the stock into various orders. After 6 p.m., when many of the office staff went home, the crooks then phoned their customers, took the orders, and had them ready to collect by about 9 p.m.

It was amazing to watch. These malingerers who seemed to baulk at the idea of hard work on company time were dashing about like mad hares now it meant they were getting an extra buck in their back pocket.

The shopping orders were piled up on the loading bay, more than ten feet high on pallets. Then it turned into *Supermarket Sweep*. Dozens of cars appeared, geezers quickly loaded up and were gone again in time for the late shift to knock off at 10 p.m.

After that, it was a nightly occurrence. The same operation kicked in like clockwork. Everyone was in on it and each one knew his role in the scam.

It didn't take long to realise why they wanted me on board. They needed a lookout. While they brazenly helped themselves to the stock, I kept watch outside in case any of the managers decided to drop by.

It was time to put my plan into action. Biggs had given me a tape recorder that the regional crime squad wanted me to use to try to gain evidence of who knew what. My task was to secure it under the shift manager's desk in the portable office that passed as the company's administrative hub.

Hiding it there in the first place wasn't that tricky. The office only consisted of a desk, a chair, a couple of telephones and some filing cabinets and was rarely manned unless the managers were meeting or someone was on the phone. What was an issue was that I had to replace the tape every night.

The safest time to do this was after 10 p.m., when the shift knocked off. Once everyone had gone, I sneaked back into the office and switched the tapes, always apprehensive that Steve or the foreman Brian would forget something and pop back in.

As the days went on, I started compiling my own dossier of who was doing what. The cops were expecting regular updates but the nightly activity meant that soon I was being swamped under a backlog of evidence.

The only thing for it was to take a day to get my reports up to date. Taking a gamble, I blew my shift and spent the day going through the tapes and getting the report sorted for the regional crime squad (RCS). I chose not to ring in sick, partly because I hadn't worked out a plausible excuse yet but mostly because I believed the shift bosses held the company in such scant regard they wouldn't care less.

Taking the extra time proved vital.

Even after only a few days recording, I couldn't believe the results. Voices I identified as Steve and Brian and some of the other leading characters on the shift could clearly be heard discussing not only who else in the shift was involved in the thefts but also an inventory of what was to be taken on those nights and who the leading benefactors of this little scam were. Together with my own evidence, they were going to give the police detailed knowledge of the crimes. Satisfied, I delivered my report to the RCS.

When I turned up the following afternoon, however, I was met with a bollocking from Steve. He tore through me, ironically blasting me for a lack of professionalism. Was this how I repaid the company's loyalty, he managed to say with a straight face.

Then it was my turn to bullshit. I explained that as I was straight out of the army and couldn't pay my maintenance for my kids, I had been nicked on a warrant and had been banged up all night in a cell. Hauled before the beak that very morning, I'd been threatened with the nick but had managed to persuade the magistrate that I now had a job and was working to pay off the arrears. If I lost this job, I said I'd told the court, I'd lose my lifeline and ultimately it would be the children who would suffer.

'I'm sorry, Steve, I bloody am,' I said. 'But if I lose this gig I'm fucked. Please, it won't happen again, I swear.'

I was sure I could see tears in Steve's eyes by the end of this sob story. By the time I made it into the cold store to continue my shift, the other lads seemed shocked to see I'd survived. When I filled them in on my Oscar-winning performance, they treated me like a hero. Then it was back to work. Christmas was on us and we were busy with the food lists again.

For a couple of weeks, I continued in the same vein. Observing as much as I could during the shift, then listening to the taped evidence in the morning and reporting it to the police. Soon, though, it became apparent that if I was going to be truly accepted into this gang I was going to have to join them in the pilfering.

In early January, I was under so much pressure to join in, some lads were starting to get suspicious I was some kind of do-gooder or worse. To save face, I helped myself to a box of apple doughnuts and three boxes of fish fingers.

I finished my shift but, by the time I was heading down the M11 to home and in the most terrible snowstorm, the van was filled with a rank smell of fish. I put my hand down near the handbrake and felt decaying soggy fish fingers that, even in the cold night, had defrosted fast. I had to get rid of them fast and had no option but to lob them out of the window.

I'd no sooner discarded a box and a half of the offending food when I saw a pair of headlights in my rear-view mirror. It was a police Range Rover from the motorway unit.

That wasn't the worst part. Even through the blizzard, I could see that the fish fingers had been hitting the cops' windscreen, the wipers smearing foul cod all over the glass.

Oh fuck, here we go, trying to explain this to a very pissed-off pair of plods.

I slowed, expecting the blue lights to flash any second. But they didn't materialise. Clearly, they dismissed it as freak conditions, overtook me and were soon lost in the whiteout. Laughing at the absurdity, I tossed out the remaining fish and, in more ways than one, breathed easy.

By late January, I had filed all of the incriminating statements to the RCS and the cops seemed so pleased with the results they decided to close the operation down. In a way, I was disappointed because I was doing so well and was almost enjoying my double role by now. But, even in the short time I'd been there, I had witnessed hundreds of thousands of profit loss to the company and it was my job to provide the means to stop it.

After a careful briefing with the RCS, it was decided that in two days they would strike the cold store. The plan was to let the thefts occur as usual that night and then with lots of local, well-hidden police back-up, they would pull all the cars over as they emerged from the factory after loading up and make the arrests.

'What's going to happen to me?' I asked.

The officers in charge looked at each other.

One Detective Sergeant said: 'We'll pick you up too – to protect your cover. Don't want to expose you as the snitch just yet.'

'That's reassuring,' I replied.

At 9 p.m. on the night of the sting, I was sitting on a forklift on the loading bay when I was called into the cold store to help bring down racks of lamb. That's funny, I thought, I couldn't remember seeing lamb on the inventory. Then I realised.

Not content with stealing their own company's stock, they'd now broken through to a meat trader's next door and were stealing that too. What a night to do it.

In an hour, the cars and vans started arriving for their deliveries and we loaded them up and sent them on their way. This was the moment of truth. Were the cops in position? Were the first arrests being made?

I waited, half expecting the shit to hit the fan and word to get back to the store what was happening. But there was nothing. It was business as usual.

Where were they? What the fuck was going on?

Now it was time for me to play my part. I'd picked a place in the middle of the convoy to leave the yard, the van packed with stolen stock.

Here we go.

My heart was beating overtime. My mouth went dry and my hands weak. I slowly slipped into first gear, wound my window down, and headed towards the main entrance up a long and bushy path. I could see nothing. No lights, no noise, nothing, as I steered left and went through the compound gate.

Then, in a flash, headlights bathed the windscreen and blinded my vision. I hit the brakes but, before the van had even come to a standstill, the door was yanked open and I was being dragged out onto the gravel road.

A stern-faced copper stood closely over me.

'I'm Ross Slater,' I whispered.

Now I'd know if the local bobbies had been properly briefed.

'Let's get you out of here,' he said. I was then handcuffed and placed in the back of a police car.

Behind me, more cars and vans were being pulled. I looked back through the side window of the police car to see mayhem breaking out and people getting tossed into vans and cars. I sat in silence as the police car pulled into the rear of the nick.

Inside the police yard, I saw the foreman, Brian, look at me and wink. I was then led into the custody office and paraded around with the rest of the detainees.

I decided to get lippy with my arresting officer and the trick worked because the custody sergeant – who clearly didn't know who I was – ordered me to be taken into a side room on my own.

There the cuffs came off and I was rewarded with a welcome cup of tea. To keep up the pretence, though, after a few minutes, I was shackled again and, in front of Brian, was bundled off to a cell. It was a further 45 minutes before the heavy steel door opened and an officer beckoned me out. I took off my shoes and followed him. My detention sheet was scrawled with the words 'Refused Charge'. I collected my belongings and walked off behind the DS into the frosty night, a free man again.

In all, 28 people across the county were arrested and charged, including Steve, the shift manager, for false accounting, burglary and theft. The next day, I went into the CIS offices to a hero's welcome. Biggs was delighted.

'Fuckin' good job, chummy. Well done,' he said, reaching into the bottom drawer for the Scotch. It was barely 11 a.m.

I savoured the praise.

'Cops happy?' I asked.

'Bloody delighted. A late Christmas present,' Biggs replied. 'Already had the DS on today. Says when they quizzed the foreman last night about you, he said, 'What him? He's new. Knows fuck all. He's not done anything wrong.'

'So there you go.' He beamed. 'Job done.'

That sentence blasted me into another world. After years out of the army, had I finally found a new calling?

In due course, all 28 appeared at St Albans Crown Court and pleaded guilty to various offences of burglary, theft and handling. I didn't even have to give evidence.

Flushed with success, I eagerly awaited my next assignment. None came. Within weeks of the Finefreeze court case, Biggs said he had a cash-flow problem to explain why he didn't think he could give me any more work.

I was gutted. I had no idea how much my undercover operation had made the firm but I was astounded. In a few short weeks, I'd gone from hero to zero.

I knew one thing though. The experience had given me a taste of what I could achieve as an undercover agent. I resolved to branch out on my own and, hungry for a new challenge, went searching for a client.

CHAPTER 3

DOUBLE AGENT

I was already awake when my phone started ringing. 7 a.m. on the dot. Just like he said.

'Chris,' I said.

'All right, Ross. Trust I didn't wake you.'

Typical ex-special forces. The hour might not quite have been the crack of sparrows but before the sun had truly risen, he sounded bright as a button. Another telltale sign that Chris was once an elite operator was the drip-feeding of information on a need-to-know basis. It had been several weeks since he'd first approached me with the offer of some lucrative work. A new client of his needed specialist tactical driving training. They would require a two-week course in covert skills, including anti-surveillance and anti-kidnap techniques, he said. My mind boggled.

'It's a sensitive client that deals in highly emotive issues,' was all he would say.

I was intrigued. The promise of some steady work, perhaps with the promise of more of the same, should things go well, was enough to whet my appetite, but my curiosity was peaked. Who could it be, I wondered?

Since I'd hooked up with Secure Services – a London-based risk-management and mitigation consultancy – I'd been handed good quality work. Run by Chris, an ex-SAS warrant officer, it was a professional outfit that attracted impressive clients. So far, he hadn't passed any chimps – as we'd say in the business – my way. I had no reason to think this particular customer would be any different.

'I'll fill you in on the details on the morning of the pick-up,' he'd said to me when he'd first sounded out my availability. Fair enough. If that was the way he wanted to play it, fine by me. I knew enough from my time in the personal protection/undercover world that discretion was always the name of the game.

My only consideration was that, if this was an international client of some renown and in need of specialist skills to help combat a very real threat, I'd have to tailor my course accordingly. It could be a real test of my abilities – but I relished the opportunity.

'Right,' he said as he continued the 7 a.m. call, 'I can imagine you'll want to know the details of today's job.'

'That would be helpful,' I said.

'It's a director for Greenpeace International, based in Brazil,' Chris said. 'She'll be waiting outside the Holiday Inn in Basildon at 9 a.m. Got that?'

'Sure,' I said, my mind already processing the information.

Greenpeace. At first, I couldn't appreciate the reason for the cloak-and-dagger approach. Sure, they dealt with emotive issues. They certainly weren't everyone's cup of tea but prejudices based on a decade with the police formed my thoughts. To coppers, Greenpeace and other green groups were just skanky veggies with their arses hanging out of their dungarees. I'd encountered their like at protests in London and times we'd dealt with them as part of the Territorial Support Group, but my appreciation of who the people were who joined their ranks stopped at the barriers that separated the demonstrators from us. It's fair to assume the police make generalisations about many groups it comes into contact with and the tree-huggers definitely fell into that category.

There was a grudging respect for their ideas and goals but little time for the methods they employed to achieve those objectives. It was them and us. The one thing that I would have said in their favour, however, is that I always found them very passive. I cannot recall a time when they were ever aggressive or violent. They were obedient – the type of protester you want when you are on crowd control. They were passionate but were not a violent protest group and in the main were well educated and respectful.

Other factors that went through my head were that this director was part of Greenpeace International – not its UK operation – and was based in Brazil. Saving the rainforests – that was certainly a cause synonymous with Greenpeace. Who were they annoying that could cause them to be kidnap risks?

Another thing that crossed my mind – this director was a woman. I had no objections there but I was curious as to what sort of battle-hardened eco-warrior I was about to come face to face with.

I might only have had two hours to get myself ready for the big meeting but I knew enough about the course I had to devise to plan ahead. I'd booked a three-litre Vauxhall Omega for the training exercises and planned to use North Weald airfield, at North Weald Bassett, near Epping Forest, as the location. It was a site I knew well. The north apron was perfect for practising tactical-driving techniques. Basically, you could throw the car around, perfect hand-break turns and perform stunts you'd be arrested for if you tried them on the open road. The surrounding area was ideal too for working on anti-surveillance skills.

At precisely 9 a.m., I arrived at the hotel and began looking for the client. There was no sign of anyone in khaki clothes and dreadlocked hair. The only person I could see outside the hotel was a diminutive woman, about 5 feet 5 inches tall, as slim as a twig, aged about 50 years old, with short grey hair. Surely not, I thought.

I pulled over to stop but, just as I was about to get out to ask if she was indeed my victim for the week, the woman casually walked over to the car and, smiling, climbed in.

Before she could speak, I said, 'I assume you're Greenpeace?'

'Yes,' she said, quite demurely, holding out her hand for me to shake it.

'Can I just say then that you'd failed the first rule of personal protection when it comes to vehicles,' I said, stern-faced. 'Never get into any old car without checking it's the right one first.'

'Oh,' she said, clearly taken aback, her hand still out, suspended in animation.

I shook it warmly.

'Right,' I said, 'let's get started. I'm Ross.'

'And I'm Alison,' she said, in a North American accent. 'Alison Barber.'

Pleased that I'd managed to break the ice and instil a measure of professionalism right from the off, I drove off to a nearby coffee shop so we could have a chat, one that would allow me to work out the parameters for the next few days. Before I commenced any course, I always made sure I established the client's level of expertise, what they hoped to achieve and, realistically, what we could achieve before the time was up.

Over a coffee, Alison explained that she was, indeed a director for Greenpeace International. Beneath her demure exterior beat the heart of a dedicated activist and she quickly launched into her back-story. Alison explained that she operated with a team in Manaus, a city in northern Brazil some 60 miles outside the Amazon jungle.

One of the main focuses of Greenpeace's action in the region was the problem of illegal logging – a global activity that costs governments hundreds of billions of dollars every year. She explained the issue affects countries in Africa, Indonesia and Russia but was particularly acute in South America and in the Amazon Basin especially, where mahogany was nicknamed 'green gold' because trading in it was so lucrative. Alison said Greenpeace – or GP as she called it – believed as much as 80 per cent of the timber trade in Brazil was illegal, and she explained how hard it was for governments and communities like the EU to clamp down on the practice because of the difficulty in tracing the origins of wood. Aside from the money it was costing governments, it was also doing untold damage to threatened forests like the Amazon. Her organisation actively tried to thwart the activities of illegal loggers by obstructing their equipment, stalling their progress and raising awareness to the problem.

However, such direct action wasn't without its risks. As logging was such big business, the illegal operators didn't take too kindly to having some environmentalists restricting their ability to make obscene amounts of cash. As you might expect, retaliation was swift and often brutal. The area manager for Greenpeace in Manaus had been the victim of numerous death threats and had been forced to move his family around several times for its own safety. Despite this, he remained committed to the cause but, as the threat levels increased, so to did Greenpeace's desire to better train their activists to stay ahead of the illegal loggers and their heavies.

People in Alison's office had already taken some measures to protect themselves, and had put into practice some rudimentary anti-surveillance techniques and operated a fleet of armoured Toyota Hiluxes with reinforced panelling and toughened glass. They couldn't take any chances because the illegal loggers' security forces were armed and wouldn't think twice about opening fire on activists. The added complication was that Greenpeace couldn't rely on the local police to help them out.

Listening to Alison talk passionately about her group's ideals and day-to-day existence, I felt myself developing a newfound appreciation for Greenpeace's efforts. She was certainly committed, made no apologies for her actions and had clearly dedicated her life to the cause. She was a devout environmentalist, up-front about her experiences with Greenpeace and open about how she got started, where she worked and when.

After our lengthy chat, I had a good idea of how to tailor the course. In some circumstances, it might have been relevant to factor in some hostile-environment training – like the military do to teach soldiers and diplomatic staff to search for IEDs, or improvised explosive devices, but I didn't feel this was necessary in Alison's case.

What she wanted to take away was a good solid skill set in personal protection and anti-surveillance. They were under a constant daily threat and she wanted to be able to feel she could look after herself.

The first task, however, was to familiarise Alison with the trickeries of driving on the left-hand side of the road. She was Canadian and had spent most of her adult life in countries that drove on the right. As we pulled away from the side of the road, I quickly realised my challenge was going to be not only getting Alison to drive on our side, but to stay on it! We had a few near misses on our way to the airfield and much of that first day was spent simply getting her accustomed to the feel of the car.

That night, I found myself mulling over all that she'd said about her situation in Manaus, so I did bit of my own research to see exactly who I was dealing with. Sticking her name into a search engine on the Internet, I discovered Alison was exactly who she said she was – a director who held a senior position within Greenpeace International. She seemed to be the person tasked with going into new countries and territories and setting up offices and putting teams in place. Once the offices were functional, she often jetted off to the next assignment.

She'd fronted up their office in Hong Kong and led protests against the Chinese on a wide range of issues, from nuclear power to waste dumping and pollution. She'd even been part of a group of protesters arrested in Tiananmen Square in 1995, for demonstrating against China's nuclear testing. Given that only six years earlier, the Chinese authorities had responded to other protesters in the same square by rolling out the tanks and opening fire, she certainly wasn't afraid of going in where it hurts.

I had a degree of appreciation for her dedication to the cause.

Over the remainder of the course, I went through with her some basic skills. We covered anti-kidnap techniques, how to avoid being followed, what to do to lose a tail, and advanced driving skills. The course I devised was one based on those I'd taken or seen in action with the police. After working hard for a few days, we then moved onto countersurveillance, driving in the wilds of eastern England, thrashing around the countryside, rounding hairpin bends, and learning all the night-driving skills at speed.

As our time came to an end, I found we had gelled in a positive way and, during breaks, we talked for hours about the work of Greenpeace. Alison also seemed intrigued by my background and she was keen to know more about my experiences, which seemed to have struck a note with her.

The final phase of the course came, and Alison enjoyed the off-road stuff, like ramming techniques and handbrake turns back at the airfield. I was impressed by how keen she was to learn and how quickly she adapted to new instructions.

I could sense a friendship developing with Alison. On our last day, we had drinks and a farewell dinner, something that didn't normally happen with clients. She asked me then about my role with Secure Services. I explained I was a freelance and I offered my services for any future training and operational matters. She floated the idea of me flying out to Manaus to see the operation she had there, with a view to me assisting her team with their training. It was an enticing proposition.

We departed and Alison went away with a fair idea of the experience I could offer and my availability. In a couple of days, she was back in Brazil but, only a few days after that, she emailed me to reiterate how impressed she had been with the skills I had taught her. She felt convinced that other senior members of her team should benefit from a similar training course, particularly those who found themselves in the direct firing line.

She had a proposition for me. How would I like to run my own courses, independently of Secure Services? The consultancy firm charged in the region of £2,000 a day for my services. I figured I could do it directly for half that amount but the suggestion presented me with a dilemma. As I was effectively starting out in the private-consultancy game, the last thing I wanted to happen was to earn a reputation for poaching work from an existing client. I'd be happy to, I told her, but only on the condition that my friends at Secure Services were happy with the arrangement.

'Leave it with me,' Alison said. 'I'll speak to them and sort it out.'

In the meantime, I requested a reference from her. At the very least, I thought it wouldn't do my portfolio any harm to have a glowing recommendation from a director of an internationally renowned organisation like Greenpeace. She duly provided one, praising me considerably. True to her word, she also spoke to Secure Services and smoothed over the transition so I was able to work for her directly.

Before long, I received a request from Dan Fleming, her logistics manager in Manaus, for the same course I'd given Alison. Already, this new-found friendship was bearing fruit, I thought. After sorting out some dates, it was only a matter of weeks before Dan arrived in Essex to be put through his paces. Dan was a rough-and-ready Scot who arrived with a solid skill set already in place. An accomplished boat handler, he was adept behind the wheel and already had a basic understanding of anti-surveillance techniques. However, he was a pleasure to work with and I was able to teach him a few tricks he didn't know.

The further positive feedback generated from Dan's time with me led to Alison swiftly following up her initial proposition. She invited me out to Brazil, to help train the volunteers in the office in security awareness, counter-surveillance and any other skills related to personal security. She suggested I spend a month out there and mentioned a large-scale training exercise they were planning in August. If I could make that, she said, I could join them on the extensive exercise in the jungle and also do my courses for the team.

It was a mouth-watering opportunity and the perfect way to enhance my credentials in the surveillance world. First, I had to run it past my boss – my wife, Carol! In the 13 years that we'd been together, she'd grown accustomed to me disappearing on various courses and assignments and, of course, there was my eight-month stint in Cairo. The added bonus from this job, however, was that I was actually being paid and, if I played my cards right, the promise of future opportunities. Unofficially, Alison had hinted that she might have a long-term plan in mind for me, one that could see me carrying out security surveys and assisting offices in other parts of the world. The idea of fitting in with their training schedule appealed to me. I made plans to go in August 2003. I was to discover that with Greenpeace, everything was very relaxed when it came to contracts and human resources. The best way of describing it was that there was a high degree of trust on both sides. Perhaps they might live to regret that philosophy.

In the intervening period before the trip took place, I busied myself with other surveillance work but, in Brazil, the situation with the illegal loggers was heating up. Campaigners hoping for an international trading ban on mahogany had been thwarted by the Brazilian government's refusal to bend to their will. Illegal logging was escalating, with the green group claiming it was responsible for depleting 15 per cent of the rainforest in the past 30 years.

An increase in the activities of the loggers meant a rise in the number of threats Greenpeace was receiving. The bandits seemed to have adopted a new tactic and were going out of their way to target the protesters, rather than thwart them as they tried to obstruct the machinery. Greenpeace activists now had to mount a rearguard action to fight them off, while at the same time trying to throw the illegal loggers off the scent of what they were up to.

Alison was feeding me regular updates but, while I was interested to hear about the latest developments, the trials and tribulations of the green activists in the Amazon basin were the last thing on my mind when I made my way to a police charity boxing match in Brentwood, organised by Special Branch. I landed an invite through my old friends at the Diplomatic Protection Group, where there was regular interaction with the guys from SB, as they are known in the trade.

These black-tie events are always raucous affairs, providing a chance for old colleagues to meet up and serving officers to let off steam. I got chatting to one of my old friends from SB, Detective Constable Terry Thomas. After the obligatory catching-up small talk, he asked if I was up to anything interesting currently.

'Been doing some work for Greenpeace,' I said.

Terry's ears pricked up.

'Really?' he said. 'What kind of work?'

I filled him in on the driving course I'd been doing but, when I mentioned I was soon to head out to Brazil, to take part in a training exercise, his eyes lit up. He was like a cat that had spotted a mouse.

'Go on,' he said, edging forward in his seat.

'Could turn into a regular thing,' I said, at that point slightly wary of where this disclosure might lead me.

We continued talking between bouts but, either I was scintillating company or it was a measure of how intrigued Terry was about my new assignment, but he suggested hanging back at the end to discuss it further over some more beers.

'So, are you involved with Greenpeace in this country?' he asked.

'No, just Greenpeace International,' I said, 'but who

knows where it might lead. If they feel I can do a job for them here, it might well lead to that.'

'Interesting,' Terry said, his brow furrowing so deeply I could practically hear the cogs turning inside his head.

It was clear Greenpeace held some interest among the law-enforcement agencies. What I didn't know at the time was that Interpol harboured a huge interest in the activities of Greenpeace. Terry had identified an area where UK cops could work with their European counterparts. Unbeknown to me, Terry set in motion a process that would transform my fortunes dramatically.

After some more beers, we left with fuzzy heads, and I didn't think too much more about it. It had been mildly surprising to see Terry's interest in Greenpeace, but it might have been just that – one cop's curiosity.

However, about ten days after that meeting, I got a call on my mobile from an unknown number.

'Ross?'

'Yes,' I said tentatively.

'It's Terry,' said the voice. 'From Special Branch. I'd like to have a chat to you about Greenpeace.'

Instinctively, I became suspicious. What did he want?

Terry explained he'd been chatting to his superiors about my involvement with Greenpeace. He asked if I could meet him and a colleague in London, to discuss it further. My mind was racing. I didn't know if their intention was to take this down an official line or was there another motive? Were they going to give me some words of advice to stay away from it? Or was it that they wanted to mine me for information?

I didn't see the harm in finding out what it was all about,

so I agreed to meet. Terry suggested the Novotel near Tower Hill station in London. It seemed a little formal for what was supposed to be an 'informal' chat, but I went along with it.

A week later, I met Terry in a room he'd booked for our little chat. This was getting more serious by the second. With him was Martin Wilson, a Detective Sergeant with SB.

Terry asked me to go over with Martin what I'd told him at the boxing meeting. Martin listened intently. After I'd finished, he said, 'Looks like there might be an opportunity here for us to scratch each other's back.'

'What do you mean?' I asked, knowing pretty well what he meant but keen for him to spell it out.

'You fill us in on everything they're up to, come on board as a covert operator.'

I looked at them. Perhaps feeling he needed to add a further incentive, Martin added, 'Of course, there will be benefits attached.'

As Martin explained further, he said SB was greatly interested in the prospect of having someone inside Greenpeace. He told me they'd had a secret operative undercover within the UK operation some years earlier, a position that had proved very fruitful. Since then, however, that source of information had dried up and they were keen to monitor the green group's activities once again.

Even although my contact so far had been restricted to Greenpeace International, this didn't seem to concern them.

'Any information will be useful,' he said. 'What their structure is, how they operate, what their targets are, who are the personnel. It's all valuable information.'

It was a lot to take in. Just a few weeks earlier, I'd been grateful for the offer of extra work from my new Greenpeace contacts and the possibility of boosting my reputation in the industry. Now, I was being asked to spy on them.

The financial reward was enticing, I couldn't deny that. Plus, my background in the army and the police meant I was more inclined to accept an offer of helping my fellow law enforcers than special-interest groups. But could I effectively betray my new contacts for a quick buck?

Martin seemed to detect my reticence.

'Think of it this way,' he said. 'Imagine these guys pull a stunt that endangers the lives of innocent members of the public. They might be well intentioned but they take it too far, cause a disruption and it all blows up in our face. Here's a chance for you to stay on the right side of the law. Do the decent thing. You won't be disrupting their plans, merely tipping us off so we know how to handle it.'

'Consider it a public service,' Terry added. 'That you're being rewarded for.'

I left them, vowing to consider their offer. I had a lot to think about. There were a number of issues, for a start. I wasn't going to be some undercover agent who was infiltrating Greenpeace, with a raft of fake ID to back up my new identity and a support team to back up my cleverly crafted cover story. My initial contact with Greenpeace had been under my real name. They knew who I was, where I lived, my background. I had to weigh up the financial benefits. Yes, it was an incentive but, was it right?

Was it better for me to carry on as before or become a double agent?

On the other hand, the idea of being retained in such a way – and by a government agency – was a potent one. An offer like this was almost unheard of. I mean, you hear of these strange things happening but I had never seen it at work. It all seemed a bit 'pie in the sky', but who knows? This could be a big break for me in times to come. It was a chance to get some undercover work – the type of role I'd craved – and at an unprecedented level. It felt very high-octane and I could feel myself getting a buzz just from thinking of all the possibilities.

I rang Terry.

'OK. I'll do it.'

I didn't want it to frustrate anything I wanted to do in my personal work. The meeting lasted 45 minutes and they gave me a contact number at SB. It was left in the air. I knew where they were if I wanted to take it up, they knew where I was. I felt loyalty to Greenpeace only in my commitment to the training. I always commit 110 per cent to the training; professionally, I would always be committed but, other than that, there was no transfer of loyalty at that stage.

'Right, what we want is everything – anything you can get your hands on – current senior figures, names and addresses, the cars they drive, their activities, ongoing and future campaigns, how they operate. We also want to know their logistics, their building construction; plus, if you can take or get your hands on as many photographs as possible, that will all help.'

It was Martin Wilson doing the talking, but my latest meeting with SB was three-handed. This time, Peter Clarke, the Detective Inspector, joined us. He wanted to reaffirm the confirmation I had given to Martin. This is how it worked in Special Branch. You were tossed up the food chain, until someone senior enough was satisfied it was all above board.

The level of information they were looking for didn't faze me. I had seen for myself the type of databases the police kept on certain groups and individuals and I knew I could add to that considerably.

When I'd phoned Terry to say I accepted their offer, I tried to set some parameters. I knew that the months following my trip to Brazil would be quiet in terms of surveillance work. It's the way it was in this business. Let's have a trial period, I told them, where they can assess the quality of information I was providing and I could establish the level of support they were willing to give me. Another factor was that, simply, I didn't know how long I would be involved with Greenpeace. I didn't want to commit to something long-term if my contact with them dropped after Brazil. They seemed happy with that.

What followed was the serious business. SB formally registered me as a covert operator – or, to give me my full title, a covert human-intelligence source, or CHIS.

When the formalities were almost done, Terry said, 'Do you want to know your new name?'

'I guess,' I said, intrigued.

'From now on, you're Chris Tucker,' he said. 'It's your file name for the Yard.'

This wasn't going to be my new identity. Nothing could get round the fact that I'd been introduced to Alison under my real name but, now I was working under the auspices of SB, I needed a file name for the use of the Yard. Any paperwork relating to the information I provided would be filed under that name. That way, the material didn't have to be officially sanitised. If I had used my own name, they would have had to sanitise every individual contact and report.

Now I had the name Chris Tucker, I was officially a source. I just had to see how much SB valued loyalty to their contacts and whether they kept their word. At the back of my mind was the experience of some high-profile sources in America whose treatment had proved the theory that over there law-enforcement agencies liked to 'use, abuse and burn' their sources. Usually, that only happened to supergrasses who received immunity in return for testifying in court against their criminal cohorts. If a source refused to testify, they'd be burned – it was often a catch-22 situation for those that turned evidence.

What gave me some comfort is that I didn't know of one covert source outside the police that had given evidence in the UK. Here, the police have a proud tradition of protecting sources, and I hoped that convention would be upheld with me. Sure, the system of procuring and funding sources had been open to abuse – most notably by the old Flying Squad of the 1970s and 1980s but, in recent times, the system had been cleaned up and rules tightened, to avoid corruption. It was a strange scenario, going from being a cop to an agent, but I can't say the transformation didn't give me a thrill and I was eager to see how my new relationship progressed.

The fact that I was an ex-cop was a big plus point and a factor in me coming on board. From the outset, SB treated me like I was still involved. They used job slang that coppers use and talked to me on their own level. I even think my file contained a note stating that I was a police source.

While Alison was in constant communication, firming up the details for my travel to Brazil, so, too, was I in regular contact with my SB handlers. We had further meetings –

two other preliminary meetings and one pre-deployment meeting. These were primarily to provide timings, flight details, where I'd be staying and when, but there were some unusual elements to establish as well.

For example, we had to work out my 'proof of life' questions. Any agencies or organisations putting personnel into situations where the risk of kidnapping is high should establish questions they can ask that only the hostage will know. Obviously, in any kidnap situation, the best proof of life is a live conversation with the victim but, failing that, it's vital to have simple, easily understood questions that can be asked through an intermediary. From training, I knew that the most straightforward ones are the best. It might be that the hostage-taker speaks limited English. However, it's good to have some back-up questions, to make sure the call isn't a hoax and to establish the hostage is still alive.

The questions I chose were the name of my first primary school and the make and model of my first motorbike – a metallic blue Pan European V-plate, if you're interested. But I had a third question that was a bit more involved. It was the question, 'Do you have eyeball?' If asked, I would reply, 'Yes,' which would lead to a supplementary question, 'Which direction?' – to which I would reply, 'Left'.

With the threat of kidnap from the illegal loggers seemingly increasing by the week, it seemed sensible to have a strategy in place. This was all well and good, but SB made it clear that, should anything go wrong, they wouldn't immediately be sending in the cavalry.

'Don't want to blow your cover, Slater,' Martin explained helpfully. 'Would just draw attention to yourself if suddenly there's a diplomatic incident because one of our agents is missing. Remember, you're a British Greenpeace worker and you'll be afforded the same degree of urgency and action as anyone else.'

The only specialist help I might get is through the intelligence agencies, Martin added. Every country has an MI6 station, so SB can work through them if there's a problem. In theory, that route is more discreet than if they contacted the embassy and raised the alarm.

I was slightly reassured by this.

The final arrangements from Alison were that I would fly to São Paulo and then transfer to an internal flight to Manaus, where Dan Fleming, the logistics manager I'd trained in the UK, would meet me, to take me to the Greenpeace office. There, my new covert life would begin.

As the day of departure approached, my head felt like it could burst with all the information I was storing and I could feel the anxiety build because of what might lie ahead. Yet, just when I thought I was tensing up and unable to concentrate on the task at hand, I relaxed and drew on my military training to calm me down. This was simply another assignment. I needed to make sure I was focused enough but also calm enough to deal with any eventualities. I reassured myself that at least I did not need a legend – the cover story that undercover agents construct to support their false identity – as I could be myself and absorb whatever was thrown at me.

The flight from London was boring and tiring but, compared to the five-hour wait I had at São Paulo before catching my connecting flight, it was a breeze. Killing time by dozing and drinking lukewarm tea, I finally boarded the internal flight and headed north to Manaus.

The first thing that hit me as I stepped off the plane was the heat. Dry, sticky and oppressive, it immediately brought me out in a sweat. By the time I collected my bag and exited the terminal building, the sun was beating down so hard I began to think I was seeing things. In a pond in front of me, pink flamingos danced around, while turtles lazed in the sun. It took a moment for me to realise this was just the local wildlife.

I was looking up and down the rows of cars outside the terminal when a dirty Hilux pulled up and the driver – a scruffy-looking bloke with stubble – leaned out, shouting my name.

I barely recognised him. 'Dan,' I said, smiling.

He jumped out and threw my rucksack into the open back of the pick-up, while I jumped into the front passenger seat. Dan gave me a hug and said, 'Welcome.' Dan was as Scottish as porridge oats and, from my experience in the army, the Jocks didn't dispense hugs lightly, so I could only imagine this was a Greenpeace thing!

Manaus – meaning 'mother of the gods' – is the capital of the state of Amazonas and is home to over 1.8 million people. I don't know if it was just the area we were travelling to, but it had the feel of an oversized town rather than a sprawling city. Much of the urban landscape was characterised by poor-quality housing and rundown districts, and I had a sense that many of the people were scraping a living. There were markets everywhere and, with the heat and dust, it reminded me of Morocco, when I visited there as a 15-year-old on board a cruise ship, to see if I might forge a career as an apprentice engineer. To me, as we made our way through the impoverished streets to the

Greenpeace office, that trip seemed like it belonged to another life to me.

Sadly, my first impressions of the city confirmed the threat assessment I'd done before leaving. After accessing the Foreign Office and CIA websites that provide useful information for travellers, I saw that it was a place where the crime rate was high, with an alarmingly high rate of gun crime, in particular. Street robberies were commonplace, along with pick-pocketing, bag snatches and gang attacks on Westerners. Welcome to Manaus, I thought, as we moved further into the urban sprawl.

I was heartened to see Dan employ some of his anti-surveillance techniques. I suspected they might have been for my benefit only, but it was good to see him cautiously doubling back on himself, manoeuvring without signalling and generally making sure he hadn't attracted a tail. The Hilux was the ideal vehicle for his needs. The glass is toughened and it has armoured plates in the sides. It could be a nightmare to drive, however, because you need more throttle to pull away and, in the wet, you need to allow three times the amount of distance time.

In a place like this, you stand out like a shag on a rock. There was no option to blend in with the locals like you could in Europe. Dan explained that, although the Greenpeace office was not publicised, everyone knew it was there. After about 30 minutes drive, we had arrived and I could see what he meant. It sat on a fairly main road, in between two low-key factories and backing on to a junior school. If you didn't know what you were looking for, I suppose you might have missed it. There were no signs or rainbow colours, but locals would have discovered immediately what type of organisation was using it.

I was immediately struck by how professional the security was. We drove up to a gated entrance with a bunker by the side, providing a good opportunity to assess the visitor before granting any access. As Dan's car was well known, we were waved through and the gate opened, but I was pleased to see that we were held in a holding area before an internal shutter-door opened. Given the all clear, we then drove into a darkened building, a welcome relief from the searing heat.

We were now in what appeared to be a huge garage, with space for up to six vehicles. Dan explained this was their logistics centre and warehouse for all their equipment. It was also home to Dan's office. It was an impressive set-up – like something the army had in Northern Ireland.

Leaving my kit behind, I followed Dan up some spiral stairs to the main office, where Alison was there to greet me like a long lost friend. A few cold drinks later and I shook hands with Roberto, the manager who headed up things here in Manaus. The guy was passionate about his work in Brazil and, from the off, he talked about how he hoped I could become instrumental in enhancing the day-to-day work in the Amazon. I could detect a true sincerity in both his actions and his voice. It wasn't hard to see how he'd clearly pissed off the illegal loggers – his actions earning him more than nine separate death threats since the office had been operational.

The office was made up of six local staff and eight other people who appeared to hail from all over the world. The manual workers who took care of the building security and maintenance of the boats and vehicles were all locally hired lads, mostly in their 20s, but really did have hidden talents, as I was to discover. They were, in fact, former Brazilian army who were expert jungle trackers and hunters, with cunning minds and the skills to match.

Even although the office staff drew from many different cultures and nationalities – Italian, Dutch, British and German – all were passionate and peace-loving people. There seemed a near-equal split of men and women, but there didn't seem to be a division of labour along traditional gender roles.

I was given a tour of the building, to familiarise myself with my new surroundings. From the open-plan office to the front of the building was a balcony and patio. It seemed a bit crazy to have an outside relaxation space given the tight security of the floor below. The office itself comprised a general meeting room with smaller private offices for Roberto and Alison off the main floor. To the left was a corridor, with a kitchen and a storeroom. If you went back to the stairs, they went up to the second floor. There, an open corridor led to a 'tech' room on the right. This was where they compiled and edited their blogs and videos. Heading down the corridor, there was a bedroom and, further down, was another bedroom, with two bunk beds, a laundry room and, lastly, another bedroom and a shower room and toilet.

While the décor wasn't exactly to my liking, the place was clean and functional. I was to be sleeping in the building and chose the small bedroom, with one set of bunk beds, overlooking the school playground to the rear. It gave me some degree of privacy and isolation, which I would need to write up my notes. It seemed almost like the VIP suite because it had a shower to itself. I took the bottom bunk. As there was nowhere to hang clothes up, I'd be living out of my bag, but it suited me fine.

After the introductions were made and I'd settled in, Alison and Roberto explained the drill to me. I would have three days to carry out my training with the rest of her staff before the main exercise with the whole group began.

Before all that, however, was a welcome party for me. They ordered pizzas and revealed a fairly large cold store of beers on the premises. It was a nice gesture, but I got the feeling that drinking and partying were a prerequisite for any committed eco- warrior. As I got chatting to the different people there, I wondered what my handlers at SB would make of all this – a tree-huggers paradise, no doubt, what with the communal living and a shared desire to change the world. They were very relaxed in each other's company. Although there was a recognised hierarchy, everyone was equal, if that makes sense? Roberto was the manager, but he was no authority figure. They were just devout environmentalists, but their cause seemed more acute out here in Brazil. It was a challenging environment and they were on the frontline. Thinking of the activists I'd encountered previously back in the UK, I began to consider that for them the frontline was a barrier at Downing Street.

Thankfully, I'd decided to hold off making any initial notes until I'd found my bearings, and I don't think they would have made much sense that first night. Several of us sat up until the small hours, drinking, and the booze, combined with the long day spent travelling and jet-lag, meant I collapsed into bed completely worn out. In the morning, I woke with a headache that would have floored Moby Dick.

I was relieved I didn't have a cover story to stick to, as I doubted I'd be able to remember anything I was saying the night before. The good thing was that the day would largely be governed by me, as I began my training for some of the staff.

I joined the rest of the group around the 15-feet table, to eat. My body was crying out for a full English, but the best I could hope for was an eco-friendly veggie-style spread. But the relaxed atmosphere, with everyone chatting and laughing and telling jokes, helped evaporate the hangover before we got down to the business of work.

Just as I was finishing eating, a big round of applause broke out and I looked up to see a newcomer arrive. He would be best described as the Birds Eye Fish Finger Captain – a crusty old sea dog with a greying full beard and tousled hair. He was Captain Bob – a legendary figure within Greenpeace. Born in Devon, he'd given up a career on British merchant ships and stumbled upon Greenpeace almost by accident. He sailed on the famous *Rainbow Warrior* – the organisation's flagship – on anti-whaling missions in the 1970s and, since then, travelled the world, taking part in campaigns and protests from over-fishing and toxic dumping to nuclear transports, climate change and war.

Although Bob's association with Greenpeace spanned 25 years and was still going strong, the same could not be said for the *Rainbow Warrior*. It made headlines around the world in 1985, when it was sunk by French agents in New Zealand, in order to stop it disrupting nuclear testing France was carrying out in Moruroa, in the Pacific Ocean.

The French agents hoped an initial explosion – caused by a limpet mine – would blow a hole in the hull, forcing the crew to evacuate. A second explosion would then sink the vessel. However, many of the crew refused to leave the stricken vessel and stayed to investigate what had happened. Among them was photographer Fernando Pereira, who was still on board when the second bomb went off. He was caught in the fast-flooding hold and drowned. A Captain Pete – Pete Willcox – was skippering it at the time. He managed to evacuate the rest of the crew.

The incident caused a national scandal, condemned by the international community. After much wrangling between the French and New Zealand governments, two agents were arrested. They later pleaded guilty to manslaughter and were sentenced to ten years in prison. They only served two before being released.

Pete had now flown in from Cornwall, to command the Greenpeace vessel *Arctic Sunrise*. The ship was one of the organisation's ice-breakers, primarily used to combat whaling in the Arctic but on this occasion was in the Amazon to assist with the forthcoming tour against the illegal loggers. A likeable and larger-than-life character, he struck me as a typical ship's captain. His word was the law and he was clearly held in some regard by his fellow activists. His arrival caused quite a stir and it was some time before everyone calmed down and refocused on the job at hand.

However, I noticed that mention of the *Rainbow Warrior* among the Greenpeace staff brought a clear change in atmosphere. It was apparent that the wounds from that disgusting show of force still ran deep.

The staff gathered in the main area, everyone from researchers to video staff to managers and the local hired help. Roberto addressed us, saying that, over the next three days, the office staff would be doing some training both in-house – and with me – and with the Brazilian security team that was arriving the following day from São Paulo. In four days, he said, we would all move down to a place called 'the Farm', a camp about fifteen feet from the edge of the Amazon jungle, to undergo extensive pre-action training. This would be interesting, I thought.

I spent the rest of my first day with Dan, on a tour of the local area to get my bearings. It also allowed me to get a feel for the place and the culture and to hear more about what Greenpeace was up against. It shouldn't have come as a surprise but the more I talked with the activists the more their commitment to the cause shone through.

At night, everyone ate together and the beers flowed once more. By the following morning, I was beginning to discover that my shower was something of a prized possession. Everyone was desperate to use it, rather than queuing for the communal block. I discovered it was quite the bargaining tool and I began trading showers for cigarettes.

Showers aside, the general protocol in the office was not a million miles from that in the army – that is, what's yours was theirs and vice versa. If you had something in your kit bag that someone needed, it seemed perfectly reasonable for them to take it and then ask your permission. I was glad I hadn't been in a fit state to make notes that first night. For the time being, at least, the logging of my findings for SB would have to wait.

That day, I began my training exercises with the local ex-military boys. They were switched on and eager to learn. They had a good grasp of English and were a pleasure to work with. I took half the staff on the first day and a half and the rest of them for the remainder of the time I had. The training consisted of situation awareness, foot surveillance and route planning. Like I'd done with the driving course, I devised the lessons based on the police system.

After the three days, I'd completed my training. We were then on to the training exercises devised by the team from São Paulo. I was intrigued as to the form they would take. I was also intrigued to meet these guys. Roberto seemed to place great faith in their professionalism. I have to admit my sense of British pride in the military training I'd received from my time in the armed forces meant I was a little sceptical as to how effective they'd be.

While we were waiting for them to arrive, the day continued with some classroom activities. At about 2 p.m., we gathered in the meeting room on the first floor, to discuss evacuation plans and how best to facilitate an extraction from a hostile environment.

Out of the blue came high-pitched screams from the adjoining office. Just as I was trying to work out what was going on …

BANG! BANG! BANG!

It sounded like gunshots. Inside the building.

What the fuck was going on?

CHAPTER 4

RUMBLE IN THE JUNGLE

The room froze.

Nobody moved, but I'm sure we were all thinking the same thing. That was definitely gunfire – and it definitely sounded like it was INSIDE the building.

My mind was going haywire. Were we under attack? Was it the illegal loggers? Why was there no alert? Where the fuck was the security?

Everyone's eyes darted around in the hope that somebody had an explanation for what was going on.

Since those initial shots, there had been nothing. The screaming had stopped and now an eerie silence befell the office. In our confined space, no one made a sound. It was like we'd all been frozen in time.

I tried to push through the initial fear and think rationally.

Who was still outside? Dan and at least one guard should be down in the bunker, while Roberto should have been in his office.

Instinct suddenly took over. I snapped into action.

'Everybody on the floor,' I shouted, as I grabbed a chair and rammed it under the door handle.

'You and you,' I said, pointing to two of the guys. 'You hold that chair in place and prop some others behind it.

My words seemed to break the spell that had been hanging over everyone. The two staff did as I asked but then others started coming out of the shock. Some of the women were on the verge of hysterics. I was about to call for calm but just then one guy – one of the researchers, not the ex-military people – made for the window. I thought he might be trying to get some air. The room was thick with tension right enough. Maybe he was going to shout for help. But, to my utter amazement, he flung open the window and climbed out. What the fuck!

Before I could stop him, he was outside and lowering himself 50 feet down a drainpipe to the ground. Christ, if I didn't restore some order, it was going to be every man for himself.

Everyone else – about 12 of them – I kept at floor level, just in case there was more gunfire through the door.

What crossed my mind was that we had been raided by locals who were being paid off by the illegal loggers and who were after Roberto – the subject of the recent death threats.

I knew we had to get out of there and the only way to find out what was happening was to have a recce outside. I gave it ten minutes and, when there was still silence, took one of the guards and edged outside the door.

At first, I couldn't see anything out of the ordinary. The office just looked deserted. Then I saw him. Oh, good God, no.

It was Roberto, lying on the floor motionless ... with a big pool of blood all around him.

He was on his side, his hand to his chest but making no noise. Holy fuck, I thought. Could it be the illegal loggers? Whatever it was, it was very real. What the fuck had I got myself into?

My instinct was to run to his aid but my military training kicked in. It had taught me otherwise. Many a soldier has been killed rushing to attend to a fallen brother. Precisely when you don't think you can afford to waste a second, is the moment to take a second to assess the situation.

I edged closer, scanning the whole office for movement and trying to detect any voices but there was nothing – it was as still as could be. The guard beside me looked in a state of shock. I left him at the door and moved towards the CCTV security-camera screens. I could see the guard hut entrance on the screen but there were no signs of anyone there. The gate was closed but the internal door was open. A nightmare situation was getting worse by the second.

At the top of the stairs was a thick steel door with heavy bolts. It was open too but I went over and shut it quickly, hastily sliding over the bolts. Still we could see no signs of intruders on the floor. Satisfied that at least we were secure on this floor, I motioned to the guard to let the others out of the room. They were like headless chickens, gasping as they stepped out onto the floor and saw Roberto's stricken body.

I went over to him. Blood seemed to be spouting out of

his back, which led me to believe there was possibly an exit wound. I felt around but could find no evidence of one. That isn't as unusual as it sounds and I carefully checked his front for an entry wound, while at the same time checking for signs that he was breathing.

I rolled him over and began emergency life support. Even though I still couldn't detect an entry point, I put a dressing on his chest and prepared to give him mouth-to-mouth resuscitation.

Just then, he sat up and smiled.

I nearly died a thousand deaths and practically jumped back about ten feet. It was like the old moving corpse in a mortuary.

This was just a bloody exercise.

'You git,' I said. 'You had me well fucking worried.'

He just grinned and got to his feet. The women looked like they had seen a ghost.

'Believable, eh,' he said, still smiling.

The blood was real, but it was pigs' blood from the market. Once I regained my composure, I watched as the mystery security company appeared. They had been hiding on the balcony. They were six of them and they were like faux special forces or those vigilante groups in America. It was all logo-embossed shirts, combat trousers and heavy boots – all black. They were armed, with guns hanging from their hips. They came out smiling, no doubt feeling like the dogs' bollocks for putting the frighteners up everyone.

I had never heard of such training by Greenpeace but, then again, we were in Brazil and the stakes and risks were not only high but were very real. I felt happy with the way

I had reacted. The measures may have been extreme but the purpose of the exercise was to show the staff what could happen when you're up against very determined adversaries who stand to lose a lot of money if you succeed with your objectives. The consequences were serious, so the training had to be serious. I was impressed. They were shock tactics but they worked. The stunt had everyone aligned to the same way of thinking. Everyone was focused. It might have been dramatic but it was effective.

When everyone had calmed down and it was established that the bloke who'd escaped via the drainpipe was alive and well, there followed an introduction from the training team. They were all ex-police or military.

Later, I sat talking to one of the team leaders and, obviously being in the same trade, we had common ground to chat over with a few beers. He explained they were a kind of paramilitary company, whose expertise was in tricky combat situations and they operated throughout South America.

After a few more beers, it was an earlier cut to bed than it had been on previous nights. The following day consisted of more training, this time in the warehouse downstairs with all of us practising embussing and debussing skills – basically how to get in and out of vehicles should we come under attack. It was useful exercise, but doing the same drill over and over again for five hours grew very tedious.

That night, I stayed off the beer as I needed to concentrate on putting together some notes for SB. I needed to provide a structured synopsis of what had happened so far, including names, faces and the methods used in their operations. The intelligence list grew longer and longer and I had to think of ways of committing this stuff to paper without it being detected. With little privacy and the danger that anyone could go rifling through my stuff, I had to think of a plan.

At around 9 p.m., I said to Dan that I needed to go into town to get some items ahead of our trip to the Farm. He warned me to be careful and gave me directions to the shops. Although the locals knew the vehicles, I asked if I could take an armoured Hilux. I put into practise my own countersurveillance moves en route and found a shop where I got what I was looking for – a large bottle of shower gel.

Back at the office, I sat in the shower room, with the water running, to dissuade any visitors. By this time, most people had gone to bed or were packing their bags for the trip to the jungle the next day.

With the noise of the shower for cover, I began writing down the intelligence I had collated to date. I took the bottle of shower gel and cut a hole in the bottom. I poured half the gel out down the plughole and, sealing my notes in a plastic bag, stuffed them inside the bottle. I then sealed the whole bottle with heavy-duty tape and chucked it in my wash bag, which in turn went into a locked bag that would be staying behind.

My thinking was that if anyone wanted to borrow the gel, it could still be used without suspicion, and without them seeing the contents inside. I hoped that scenario would not happen.

Only a skeleton crew was left at the office when the rest of us departed for the trip to the Farm, on the edge of the Amazon jungle. The camp was approximately 70 miles from Manaus, but it seemed to take an age for our convoy of pickups and cars to make the journey. In all, with the addition of some volunteers, there were around 30 of us.

We arrived in total darkness, not being able to see anything except a dimly lit cookhouse in the distance. Following the shapes in the dark, I arrived at the cookhouse to get a much-needed coffee. The security company arrived and seemed to be heavily armed, and a lot of talk was buzzing around the camp. I learned the police had circulated details of an escaped prisoner from a nearby prison, hence the upgrade in arms. This time it was no joke.

The Farm was essentially a camp about a quarter of a mile squared, comprising of three wooden tree houses at one end and the cookhouse at the other with a swimming pool and picnic area in the middle. The boundary of the jungle was just 30 feet from the tree houses. With the forest location, combined with the stifling heat, it felt very much like we were in the jungle itself.

Although we'd been briefed that we would be here for a few days, we had no idea how long this would actually mean or what form the training would take. Initially, we were told our accommodation would be in the cookhouses but then the head honchos had a change of mind and realised that's where the training staff would be sleeping, so we were shunted to the tree houses.

Part of the plan was clearly that we were to be segregated. I anticipated more fun and games from our trigger-happy friends in the combat gear. Some members of the training team were milling about, so I assumed that we would be taking part in an exercise under their supervision.

Roberto seemed to take a sudden dislike to the sight of the firearms flaunted by the security company – a marked change from his attitude at the office during the last exercise. The show of weaponry didn't fit with Greenpeace's peaceful image.

I left at this point and headed to my bunk. The accommodation was up on the first floor and off the walkway that ran round the entire circumference of the block. Everything – the floor, stairs, bunks and walls – were made of wood. If a fire had broken out, we would have gone up like a tinderbox. Inside the tree houses, the rooms were 15 feet square, with four bunks squeezed in and precious little space for anything else, including people. You couldn't move in there. The heat was so intense and, after the monotonous drive up there, I dived into the shower to try to cool off. When I came back, one of the guys in the bunk next to mine was sitting there, doing his boots up. There was not one spare square inch. I had to wait until he was done before I could get in. By the time I did, the water droplets on my back had been replaced by new sweat. Right then, I thought this was going to be some test of endurance in the camp.

The tightness of the space just added to the oppressive atmosphere that had already been created by the guns and the word of the escaped prisoner. After the relaxed joviality of the office, we now found ourselves being tested in every way. Right from the off, the setting was very uncomfortable and unsettling. It was a situation ideal to wear you down. Everything was pressurised – the space that you lived in, where you could go, the times we ate. Everything was dictated. There was such a feeling of claustrophobia, it made me think of the training reserved for special forces. It was a mental wearing-down process from the minute we had arrived. Even during that first night, squabbles started breaking out between people I'd previously pegged as peaceable and chilled out. After the escapades back in the office, everyone was on edge, waiting to see what the next exercise would be.

Trying to get sorted in a small room with four other blokes in the dark was a nightmare, and the added feature of bats flying around your head did nothing to inspire a good night's sleep. Eventually, I gave up and rolled out a sleeping bag and dropped off for the night.

Four hours later, we were woken up and the training team launched straight into lessons on navigation in the jungle, where we learned all about how to find your way about in the darkness without any discernible landmarks to guide you. This took place in the next hut, so we didn't have to go into the jungle, but the early start was all part of the disorientating process, I thought.

When that short exercise was over, it was time for breakfast. After a broken night's sleep, some of the team were getting even tetchier. I quickly realised it was a deliberate ploy. This was an old-fashioned technique of wearing us down gradually to place us under pressure to make wrong decisions. The old tricks are always the best but in this case they were deemed vital. If the illegal loggers captured any of these activists, they'd be put through hell. It was better to give them a taster of that discomfort in these surroundings, rather than them finding themselves up to their neck in without any clue as to how they'd handle it.

That morning, we were set exercises for the day on jungle preparation. These covered map-reading, using compasses, basic jungle-survival techniques, emergency rendezvous points, all laying the ground for the time when we entered the jungle itself.

By lunch, many of the group were flagging so much that we barely reacted when we all sat picking over a basic meal of rice and fruit and, out of nowhere, seemingly, something rolled off the roof of the cookhouse straight onto the seat opposite me. It was a snake! The sight of the slithering reptile – whether poisonous or not – caused some of the guys to throw their food and run.

If anything, their reaction only served to calm me and I stayed seated, watching the animal to see what it did.

While many of the guys jumped around like nervous kittens, one of the trackers just sat there silently and produced from under the table a flash of steel so quick I saw it only as a blur. He had sliced the head of the snake clean off and the knife was put back as quickly as it had appeared. Apparently, it was a very poisonous young snake and its family were close by, so we needed to be careful.

The young tracker then picked up the snake's body, placed his fingers right where the cut had been made and squeezed hard. A creamy white glue-like substance dripped out of it. This was the venom. As some of us sat agog and those that had been jumping around calmed down, the trackers eventually stopped laughing at our reactions.

If it hadn't crossed my mind before, I was now realising this was about the strangest undercover job I could ever have imagined. Once order had been restored, we regrouped and went back to our activities in preparation for our jungle expedition.

At night we tried to settle down and get some sleep, all

the time wondering when the training company were going to spring into action with another of their stunts. We didn't have long to wait.

CHAPTER 5

TURNING UP THE HEAT

The second I came to I knew something was up.

If the commotion of people banging around on the walkway outside my room didn't arouse my suspicions, then the dirty big blast from the direction of the jungle certainly did.

What the hell was that?

In seconds, I was up and dressed and out on the walkway trying to assess the situation – something that was easier said than done in the pitch darkness. It was 3.30 a.m. My first instinct was that it was a genuine attack. Gunfire now ripped through the blackness, swiftly followed by ear-piercing screams from down below.

Don't tell me the camp has been breached.

Dan was on the balcony lobbing anything he could find down below to try to put off any potential attackers.

'What the hell's going on!' I shouted.

'Fuck knows,' he shouted back. 'But I'm not taking any chances.'

Just then, another explosion lit up the sky. For a split second, everything was bathed in bright light before the night swallowed up the camp once more. In that brief moment, however, although I'd detected a lot of running about down on the ground, no one was actually making any attempts to come up the ladder.

To me, that was a telltale sign that it was an exercise – that and the fact that no one was shouting that there were casualties.

'Sounds like another exercise,' I said to Dan.

'Sounds bloody real, if so,' he replied.

I couldn't argue with that. If this was simulation, it was bloody impressive. Another explosion, this time on the other side of the tree house. More shouting, more gun shots. Whoever was behind this clearly wasn't going to be happy until every piece of activists' underwear was well and truly soiled.

It was easy to get scared in situations like this. That was obviously the idea – to test reactions. Sometimes, though, the fear overrides common sense and logical thought. Logical explanations don't register when you are panicking. There were women in the tree houses and they were hysterical.

It's OK, I figured, it's only part of the training. The explosions continued. The military pyrotechnics carried on for about an hour and then all of sudden everything died down. There was no signal to return to our beds but I felt confident enough that this was yet another attempt to destabilise us.

I tried to reassure the others that it was all part of the game but some of the guys weren't having it. It's funny to observe what some people will do in a panic situation but I surprised to see some of them trying to bring down washing that was hanging up over the balcony. As if you'd stop to do that in a real assault situation.

No sooner had I put my head down than the fireworks started again, about half an hour after the original cessation. This time, it was continual, there was shouting and gunfire. People were running about the tree houses, shouting warnings not to go to a certain side because people were there. For a moment, I wondered if this was indeed real but, like earlier, there were no abduction attempts or any efforts to raid the tree huts so I felt sure we were safe.

This was doing nothing for my beauty sleep, however.

The disruption went on for some time and was proving very effective in scattering the activists and making them agitated. To be fair, it is quite alarming to be exposed to gunfire, the smell of smoke and people screaming for a sustained period of time and not to know exactly where it's coming from or who's making all the noise.

Unfortunately, for those of us keen to get some shut-eye, this was now going to be the habit for the rest of the night. Every time we did a head count, got back to bed and tried to close our eyes, it would start up again. Some people got so fed up, they started sleeping in hammocks outside on the balcony, just so they wouldn't have to go through the rigmarole of getting up again.

Despite the lack of sleep, this was shaping up to be one of the best training exercises I'd been on. Everything was so relevant to the dangers the activists might face and it was expertly executed. The pyrotechnics alone must have cost hundreds of pounds.

In the morning, we were up bright and early again, to continue our training. Living a commune-style existence took a bit of getting used to, as I discovered when I wandered into the shower block to find two women already in there. Feeling embarrassed for them that I had stumbled in, I began to apologise, but they weren't bothered in the slightest. Clearly, the live-and-let-live spirit from the movement's hippy origins was alive and well. I wondered, if only fleetingly, how far they took the free-love spirit!

That day, we split up into groups, for a controlled walk into the trees, to put into practise the jungle craft we'd learned. We were shown how to obstruct the loggers' machinery. Clearly, the tactics employed didn't involve confrontation with the loggers themselves, more trying to cause them disruption. It was a strategy that seemed to work for them.

We later learned what passed for edible food in the jungle, which animals you could eat and which would give you a dodgy tummy, at best. The trappers also taught the activists some rudimentary fishing and trapping techniques.

Towards the end of the day, we were to split into groups and ventured out into the Amazon jungle. Now this, I was looking forward to. I'd done similar things with the military, although I had to admit the English countryside had nothing on the weird and wonderful creatures I might be expected to meet in the Brazilian rainforest.

So, come 5 p.m., we left the camp, climbed a wire fence and wandered straight into the Amazon. All around us was an amazing array of sights and sounds. The jungle really did

Left: Ross Slater during service in Berlin with 2 Para during the Cold War in the 1970s.

Inset: Slater's close friend Corporal Paul Sullivan with daughter Alesia. Paul was killed in action at Goose Green in the Falklands War.

Right: The lead co-ordinator of the Greenpeace office in Istanbul.

Above: Greenpeace planning a briefing pre-action stage.

Inset: Slater with the police's Territorial Support Group in London, preparing for an outbreak of public disorder.

Below: An activist and head of a Greenpeace nerve centre in Istanbul, Turkey – also an expert in honey-trapping.

Above: In Turkey, where planning and preparations take place for actions in the Mediterranean region.

Below: Tracking marine targets and intelligence-gathering.

The Greenpeace international roping team.

Above: Training in confrontation and Protests through NVDA (Non-Violent Direct Action).

Below: Mission planning with Greenpeace's international boat squad.

Greenpeace lead roping
instructor deliberates during
a day of training in Turkey.

Above: The research and Intelligence team at Woodyville works late into the night to piece together a briefing for an exercise.

Below: Ross Slater in a covert reconnaissance role on a target in the south-west of the UK.

Above: The roping team lectured in the art of a rope rescue of a fellow activist caught up during a rope decent.

Below: Ross Slater in the Ukraine honing weapon skills during operations.

seem alive and my ears rang with the cacophony of noise from birds, insects, frogs and other tree life. Our tracker, Juan, seemed to feel his way through the undergrowth, while some of us less-experienced jungle-dwellers picked our way through, tripping on every second tree stump. Hacking our way through the undergrowth, we trekked for nearly two hours, but it was impossible to tell how much progress we'd made in that time.

By the time we stopped for a well-earned rest break, I felt a good ten pounds lighter from the amount of sweat dripping off me. Refreshments were in short supply, but Juan showed us how to strip off some tree bark to access some water underneath. It was like the sweetest nectar I'd ever tasted, after my recent exertions. We rested for quarter of an hour but, in that time, we were being bitten so badly by insects we were all ready to keep moving. We ploughed on for another hour but, by this time, the light was all but faded and it was time to make camp for the night.

We made makeshift hammocks in the trees. Mine was comfortable enough but, despite my tiredness, sleep was a forlorn hope. Juan had given us mosquito nets, but it offered little in the way of protection. I spent a restless night swatting away insects, feeling as though I was being eaten alive, with the sound of crickets now a deafening crescendo.

At 4 a.m., after achieving the most shallow of dozes at best, I got up and joined Juan and the rest of the group as we continued our progress through what seemed like a thickening undergrowth to our ultimate destination. Eventually, we arrived at a clearing in the rainforest. The site was about 120 feet square and could have passed for any normal jungle clearing – but for the mass of mechanical equipment that littered the forest floor. There was a log shredder and a compressor/processor machine for sterilising the bark before it's transformed into transportable loads.

The site itself and the machines had clearly been used – relatively recently, according to the Greenpeace guys – and, although it did not perform a core role in terms of activity, it was thought to be one of many scattered around the Amazon that provided satellite facilities for the illegal operators in addition to the main logging plants. Although the machines were rusty in parts, they could have been reutilised with some minor servicing.

The hulking machinery made for an incongruous sight, given the natural environment from which we'd just emerged. Juan explained illegal loggers often abandoned these cutting devices, either because they were too costly to move or because the loggers had moved temporarily to another location. The whys and wherefores weren't Greenpeace's concern, however. It was a good opportunity for the activists to obstruct the machines so, should the illegal loggers return, they would be unable to continue their business as usual. As the group pondered ways of frustrating the work, I suggested an easy way would be to knacker the engine mechanism by unbolting the flywheel and taking out the shaft.

No sooner had I suggested it than everyone looked at me. For a split second, I weighed up what I was about to do. I'd begun my association with Greenpeace as security adviser and training consultant. It wasn't as if I'd signed up as an activist. Yet, here I was about to disable property that didn't belong to me for a political cause.

In terms of SB, I was already an activist. Simply by

turning up at a demo with this mob would qualify me in their eyes. Suggesting and undertaking direct action might muddy the waters, however. I wasn't an undercover cop on a covert mission but, was I crossing the line by getting involved? Should I make some excuse and risk blowing my cover?

I pondered the dilemma for about two seconds. Then I calmly took off the flywheel. In for a penny, in for a pound, I guess.

We spent another night in the jungle. By now, the constant heat, the insects and the lack of sleep were wearing us all down. If I needed any more convincing that these guys were dedicated to their cause I witnessed it on those testing few days at the camp, and in the jungle.

The following morning, Juan led us to another sight you don't expect to see in the middle of the Amazon – a car park. It might not have been the multi-storey NCP blocks we're used to seeing back home but, the presence of several open-backed trucks and an old 4x4 was enough to jolt us back into reality.

Any suggestion that they belonged to sightseers or local farmers was quickly dispelled when one of the office staff checked the registration numbers against a database they had. They all matched those on a list of those belonging to illegal loggers. Crouching in the undergrowth, we scanned the vehicles and the surrounding area for signs of life. There was none.

In the far distance, we could detect the faint sound of a plant in operation. Whether that had anything to do with the cars we had here, no one knew. Again, however, this was an opportunity no self-respecting activist is going to pass up.

We set about the vehicles, once more the motivation being to frustrate their efforts. They were seen as fair game.

I was now almost enjoying being part of the action, being one of the agitators. For years, I had been on the other side of the barrier, curiously observing and to a small extent judging the people who campaigned and protested. Now, a part of me felt like one of them. At the same time, however, I felt excited about the quality of the information I would soon be passing on to SB. So this is what it felt like to be a double agent.

Job done, we all headed back to the Farm, a trip that required yet another night under the stars. By the time we staggered into the camp a day later, I felt like I'd been eaten alive. Living on scraps for three days, I was desperate for a proper meal and consoled myself that, over the last few hours before we arrived, the cooks would have something waiting for us.

We arrived to be told by the security team that the food had been stolen and we only had bread and water for the next day or so. Great!

After a meagre snack, I sat on the walkway at the top of the tree house and watched the sun set over the trees. From my vantage point, I spied two of the security guys sitting outside tucking into sausages, fruit and drinking what looked like coffee. So much for the food being stolen. Yet another attempt to destabilise us, I thought. I could sense more fun and games to come.

I showered and collapsed back in the bunk. After the arduous three days I'd had, I was ready for sleep and imagined I'd snooze through anything the security mob tried to throw at us. I was expecting another light show but

I was confident I wouldn't give them the satisfaction of seeing me rattled.

I had drifted off for little less than twenty minutes when I was jolted from my slumber by the other teams who were late back came from their jungle expedition.

Stomping through they came, causing a right commotion and waking everyone up. That's it, I thought. Sod not showing my frustration. Enough was enough. I got up and, as everyone looked on bemused, made a hammock outside on the walkway. Let the others get on with crashing about in the bunk rooms. In the short term, it was a good move. I managed to eke out about three hours sleep.

BANG!

Another explosion awoke me with a jump. The sky was lit up with flares. Gunfire crackled through the camp below. It was another simulated attack, I was sure.

I was still trying to come to my senses when people started barging into my hammock. What the hell?

I scrambled to my feet. Luckily, I was half dressed and quickly able to sort myself so I could begin to work out what was going on.

All around me, voices were shouting out in foreign languages. Greenpeace activists were cowering down under the shelter of their bunks. Dan was back on the balcony, this time barricading the stairwell. The security company was trying to breach the tree houses.

Nerves frayed through lack of sleep and empty stomachs, those of us still in the tree house tried to keep down, assessing what was happening. It certainly did seem an escalation in the intensity from the first night but, again, in the absence of casualties and the time it was taking for anyone to actually come up the ladders, I reassured myself that this was more simulation that would eventually pass.

I retreated to my bunk and, through sheer exhaustion more than anything else, collapsed and closed my eyes. Despite the pandemonium going on around me, I drifted off. Time and again, I woke to hear the same explosions and fuss around me.

Curse these bastards, I thought. Did they never give up?

Clearly, the intention was to drive us all nuts, pit us against each other and have our tempers and nerves shredded so much, we'd all come down screaming for it all to stop.

There were signs it was working. By 4.30 a.m., the tree hut was a mess and people were walking around like drugged puppies. Some had already gone during the night – where to I had no idea. It must have been while I was sleeping. Those that were left some were planning an escape. It was really a case now of survive or fall. All of this seemed unreal for a peace group but, as I reminded myself, this was South America and situations like this had happened in the past. The trainers from the security company were turning up the heat, but not for the first time I was beginning to think they were over-zealous with their handling of young, inexperienced activists in their charge.

I tried to remain calm. I went back to my bunk, kicked off my shoes and lay down once again.

Just then, gunfire exploded into the early dawn. I thought it was only seconds later but, when I looked at my watch, it was 6.30 a.m. Christ, where was everyone? My room was empty and I couldn't hear anyone moving around outside.

My head was buzzing. Lack of sleep and food, the

oppressive heat and the constant barrage of noise throughout the night had played havoc with my senses.

I could hear men shouting in foreign accents on the ground below.

Here we go again, I thought, trying to convince myself this was still more of the same tactics. Something told me, however, that this was different. Focus, I told myself. I hauled my boots on, barely pausing for the now customary check for bugs first, and made for the door of the room, rubbing my eyes and head to try and wake myself up.

BANG! BANG! BANG!

Christ, more gun shots. Now I was awake. Through the night the firing seemed almost abstract, a distant sound effect purely for show, with no real intent. Now, though, it seemed targeted – very real – and, unless I was mistaken, directly below my tree hut.

This was still an exercise, right? Still a game?

Where the fuck was everyone? What had happened in those last two hours while I'd been out?

I was trying to answer these questions when something made me hit the floor.

Suddenly this didn't seem like a game any more.

We were under attack.

CHAPTER 6
AMBUSHED

The sound was unmistakable. Even in my disorientated state, I was sure it was a woman's scream. I tried to locate the noise but my senses were working overtime. Then it came again and, this time, was accompanied by frenzied foreign voices and the sounds of a violent struggle. It was directly below me.

'No! Stop!' She was speaking in English but what she'd said next was stifled and muffled, like something or someone had blocked her mouth.

My instinct was to go for the door. But, wait, was it a trap? How I could be sure this wasn't another set-up? I'd be playing into their hands. It would look like I hadn't learned anything after all the days of intense training we'd had.

But, what if this was real and she was in trouble? What if the illegal loggers whose equipment we'd disabled had tracked us back to here? Could they have launched a genuine attack at the same as the security people were staging theirs? How could I live with myself if I sat back and did nothing?

She screamed again. God, it seemed bloody real. My mind flashed back to the incident in the office. Then, it had been a short burst of activity, the set-up to Roberto's simulated shooting and then an examination of how we reacted and handled the extreme pressure.

This seemed much more prolonged. And, if this was a set-up, where was the audience? Where the hell was everyone else? I remembered seeing some people make a run for it during the night but if everyone had evacuated or thought enough was enough and congregated in the cookhouse, why would they go to such lengths to smoke out the rest of us? Was I the only one left standing? This couldn't be for my benefit, could it?

Bloody hell. What was it with these people?

For a moment, there was silence. In my confused state, I wasn't even sure I could still hear the jungle. It was like someone had turned off the chorus of crickets and other wildlife.

Then it came again. The same woman, crying, more muffled this time but clearly in pain, by the sounds of it. Surely, they weren't torturing her? If this was a game, it sounded bloody real. What the fuck was going on?

Angry foreign voices were barking what seemed like instructions directly below the tree house where I was now cramped motionless, not wanting to give away my position.

They seemed to be shouting questions now. I couldn't make out what they were saying but I had a good guess. Are you alone? Where are the others? Even if this were still a simulation, it would follow the same form as a genuine raid.

I had to make a decision. In some ways, it didn't matter if this was still an exercise or we were being attacked for real. My responses had to be the same. I had to tough it out. I couldn't take any chances.

If they'd got the girl, the next place they'd search was this room. There was only one thing to do. I couldn't risk blowing my cover.

Frantically, I looked around the room. There was nowhere to hide. Not for the first time since I'd arrived in the camp, I cursed the sparseness of the huts. Hiding underneath one of the bunks seemed my only option. I'd be discovered in a second.

Then I had an idea. The space hardly looked big enough to squeeze into but it had to be worth a go. If I was going to attempt this I had to move fast.

Creaking on the slats of the ladder below made my mind up for me. It was time to act.

As silently as I could, I crouched and crept underneath the floor planks in the room. There was just enough space for me to squeeze under them and lay between the floor and the structure holding the entire thing in place on the tree.

What was happening outside? Had someone come up? I could still hear sounds of scuffling below, a struggle perhaps. Was someone being dragged somewhere? The noise was making it hard to detect if anyone was now up in the tree hut itself.

My heart was racing, the sweat gushing from every pore. If my brain was trying to tell myself this was all still a game and it didn't really matter if I got caught, my body certainly wasn't listening. The old feelings I'd last experienced in the army came flooding back.

I tried to control my breathing, to ease my movement in the cramped space. Then, just as quickly as they'd started, the sounds of struggle subsided. The voices fell away. Whoever it was that had been grabbed was most likely being abducted to another location.

I started to think perhaps no one had come up stairs.

Then, suddenly, I heard footsteps. It sounded like they were coming from the balcony just outside the room I was under. My heart was beating so loudly, I felt sure they'd hear it. The footsteps stopped. They must have been right at the door. I thought my heart would burst from my chest. It took every ounce of energy to keep still my panicking breath. After what seemed like an age, the footsteps began again and, to my intense relief, appeared to be moving away from my hiding place. I breathed out.

Still, however, I couldn't be sure what was out there. Fearing the silence outside was some sort of trap, I waited nearly an hour before finally summoning the resolve to move. By the time it came to emerge from under the floorboards, it took the greatest effort to command my limbs to function, so cramped had they been in the confined space.

I slipped out of hiding and, fearful that the boards would creak and betray my position, I walked slowly on the sides of my feet to avoid putting my full weight on the wooden flooring underfoot.

I tried to assess what was happening. If this was still a training exercise surely they'd overstepped the mark. It felt more like an initiation to the SAS than to an environmental group. Had they lost their minds? But what if it wasn't an exercise? What if bandits had raided the camp and the screams I had heard were real? These young activists could have been raped and abducted. What the hell had I got myself into?

I slowly crept outside the room and onto the balcony. I had a great vantage point but I couldn't see anyone. There seemed no movement anywhere. Given the bustling hive of activity the Farm had been since we'd arrived, it was eerie to see it so still. I tried to weigh up my chances. If this was still the work of the security company the chances were they'd know I was still up here. They could just wait for me to come down. Illegal loggers, on the other hand, or the heavies they probably employed to warn off the likes of Greenpeace – wouldn't know how many people were here, so would most likely leave once they'd felt they'd meted out some sort of retribution for yesterday's activities.

What were the chances of them finding this place? It wasn't a Greenpeace location and wasn't a site used by the organisation, or any other environmental group to launch action plans. Could they have followed us here? Did they spot us disabling the vehicles?

God knows.

The only thing I knew was that I had to explore the rest of the camp to see who else was here. Were our vehicles even still here? Wouldn't that just be my luck – stranded in the Amazon, with no idea how to get back to civilisation.

As silently, but quickly, as I could, I moved towards the ladder, trying desperately not to cause the wood to creak unnecessarily. On the ground, I'd at least have some cover around the edge of the camp.

At the top of the ladder, I crouched down to see where to go next once I got to the ground. I was trying to work out the safest course of action when – WHACK! – my head exploded. My face hit the wood. I tried to coordinate my senses but my mouth was clogged with dirt and dust, my eyes stung and my brain buzzed like an out-of-tune radio. The only thing I was conscious of was a terrible stench of sewage as a coarse dark hood was wrestled roughly over my head. The cloth made me gag but as I fought for breath and the hood caught in my mouth my arms were wrenched behind me up towards my shoulder blades and tied behind. Before I could struggle free, my legs were bent back up towards my backside and my ankles shackled.

My mind scrambled as I tried to work out how many attackers were on me. My face was pushed further into the dirt as I felt a man on top of me. He must have been kneeling on my back pushing the last breath from my body.

'Who are you?' a voice hissed in my ear. 'Where are the others?'

Even if I'd wanted to reply, I couldn't, but the broken English couldn't be from an illegal logger, could it? This still had to be a simulation, hadn't it? A very real, bloody scary simulation.

I stayed silent and pretended to be unconscious, pretty plausible given the force with which they threw me face down on the ground. Suddenly, I remembered my military training. Think of something calm, something safe, amid this chaos.

My head was spinning. The simple act of trying to recall something made it near impossible. Think, Slater, think. Then it all came back. Harriet's birth – my first-born child.

She and my other two children were my reason for living. God, I needed them now. There were other voices now nearby. Several of them were barking orders all around me but I had a vivid recollection of being handed this helpless baby for the first time. Instantly, I felt a wave of calmness wash over me, ridiculous given the circumstances. Who'd have thought those ball breakers in the Paras knew what they were talking about?

I almost smiled as my mind wandered to Aldershot and the lads I trained with. But then I was dragged by my ankles. My face scraping off the uneven planks of wood.

The barks continued to come, this time in a language I couldn't understand. Maybe a good thing as it stopped me getting riled – well, any more than I already was. Then I was being lifted. Four men it seemed, one with each leg and arm. Christ, was I going to be thrown down the stairs?

Keeping my eyes shut, I tried to brace myself but, mercifully, my captors carried me, albeit roughly, down and then dumped me on solid ground outside.

Mumbling, I curled into the foetal position expecting the kicks and punches to come. Instead, I heard the noise of a vehicle growing louder. The vibrations in the earth told me it was coming straight for me. At the last moment, it halted right by my side, showering me in dust and earth. I felt my bladder weaken. God, not now. If I pissed myself in this situation, they'd know how terrified I was. I clenched but didn't know how long I'd be able to keep it in.

Again the voices started and I heard a handgun being racked back near to my ear.

BANG!

The gun went off seemingly inches from my head. The

noise exploded in my skull and it took every ounce of energy to hold my position.

There followed a further three shots. Clearly designed to panic me, it was doing a good job. My nostrils filled with the unmistakable smell of burned cordite. But my mouth was so dry and stale that the familiar scent, however terrifying, was like honey on my tongue.

Without warning, I was lifted again, this time higher and I felt myself being half thrown, half shoved onto a metal ledge. The back of the truck, I guessed. Bloody hell, what now?

The vehicle took off and, blind to the direction of travel, I rolled from side to side. After a few moments, I grew accustomed to the jolts and figured we weren't going anywhere. It felt like we were going round in circles.

Eventually, the truck seemed to straighten out and stop. I was hauled out of the back and thrown down to the ground. There was noise all around me, and I could hear the sound of metal crashing and the dragging of something nearby, which suddenly stopped.

Now there were shouts in broken English.

'Who are you?'

'Who your friends?'

Still hooded and face down, I stayed silent.

Then it was up and I was put on what felt like a stretcher. I was just trying to work out if my surroundings had changed when – *splash* – a bucket of water was thrown over my head.

Fuck! The water gushed through the hood and soaked my head. I scrambled from my position, trying to tuck my head in and get some air to breath. It felt like I was being submerged. Another bucket of water came down, then another.

Christ! Who were these cretins?

I was struggling to breath. As I hunched up, the hood tightened around my neck and I felt myself suffocating. I started to struggle. Panic took over.

I was spluttering and coughing.

Then someone pulled the hood away from my mouth and I felt the air rush in. God, I'd never welcomed anything so much in my life. I gulped huge lungfuls. When eventually I calmed and my heart slowed to only a million beats per minute, I realised I was alone. There was no one around.

I was still hooded but couldn't detect any movement around me. It was just me and the stifling heat.

Only then did I notice I had wet myself. In the panic of the water torture, I'd let myself go. Still, I mused, with the drenching I'd taken, no one would notice the difference.

There was little respite from the torture. Again came the sound of commotion. The people were back. Still on the stretcher, which felt like the old canvas ones we used in the army, I was carried a short distance but indoors. Cool air replaced the claustrophobic heat.

Whoever was doing the carrying laid me, more gently this time, on a cold floor. The relief was amazing.

More questions came. The same as before. Still I remained passive. One said, 'You want to sleep on a bed?'

I didn't answer. I was lifted and dropped onto a set of bare bed springs. Fuck, that hurt, as several sharp spring ends dug into my groin. I let out a dull moan but said nothing.

Then after a minute or so, I heard a little voice whisper,

from where I couldn't tell. It said, 'How are you? You OK? It's me.'

I said nothing. This was a trick, I knew. A so-called friendly voice to engage you in conversation and reel you in.

It came again, louder this time, but still friendly. 'It's me. Listen, are you OK? Talk to me.'

I hadn't held out this long to fall for this now.

The door suddenly opened and in walked several people, all talking in the same foreign language. They seemed to be carrying someone else out all the time, making different noises as if to disorientate me. I continued lying there for what seemed an eternity, trying to focus on the things I'd be enjoying when I finally got out of this mess – a cold beer, playing in the garden with my family. It is strange that such simple thoughts can give so much comfort when your back is against the wall.

I tried to think logically. Instead of loggers or the security company, could this actually be Greenpeace? Had they twigged I was spying on them? This was so far removed from the cuddly image of the tree-huggers most punters had of them.

I tried to retrace my actions. Had I given anything away? I was sure I hadn't. I was still at the information gathering stage. Had someone back at the office gone through my stuff and found the shower gel bottle? Could they have found my notes and relayed a message to the leaders at the camp?

If that was too far-fetched an idea, then what was this?

By now, I found it hard to believe this was still an exercise. It was all too extreme, too real.

Illegal loggers? Seemed plausible. Wouldn't that just be my luck? Kidnapped by the very people I'm being trained to evade. Either way, it was a cluster-fuck of massive proportions.

The door opened again, and I was carried outside. I heard laughter and joking from where people sounded like they were eating and singing. Finally, someone said, 'Hey, it's Slater. You not joining us then?'

The hood was yanked off.

'It's over,' Juan, my tracker from the day before said, as my eyes blinked and tried to focus.

I breathed out and clambered to my feet, gingerly, while the sensation returned to my aching limbs. I was in a glorified hut just yards from where everyone else from the group was sitting by tables many of them smiling at me.

I was helped to a table where Dan and most of the guys were. I just sat there stunned and numb, trying to orientate myself to the environment again.

I tried to get my head around the fact that this had all been an exercise. No one was hurt. Everyone was safe. It had been a test to see how we handled extreme stress. Apparently, I passed. It was only later that I discovered that the whole exercise, including my detention and torture had lasted 17 hours.

A man, who I later discovered was the boss of the security company, came over later and hugged me.

'You did bloody well, my friend. Here, have this. A token of our respect. For all your trouble.'

He presented me with a company polo shirt. A bloody polo shirt. Some 17 hours of torture and they expect me to wander around advertising these psychopaths?

I wanted to tell him where he could shove it.

CHAPTER 7

THE INNER CIRCLE

'Come on in, Ross, the water's lovely.'

It was Clara, one of the Dutch women, in the pool – and joined by everyone else.

Just a couple of hours earlier they had still feeling the effects of a training regime that would have tested even the SAS. Now they were skinny-dipping in a pool on the edge of the Amazon like tourists on some exotic eco-warrior Club 18–30 holiday!

'I don't have anything to wear,' I protested, knowing full well this wouldn't wash as an excuse.

'Neither's anyone else!' She laughed.

A barbecue was in full swing. It was dusk on the last night in the camp and everyone was clearly letting off steam after several hard days. I had been feeling a bit pissed off at the level of treatment I'd received from the security team but it's amazing what the sight of a few beers, the smell of burgers cooking on a grill and the sight of a pool of naked people will do to snap you out of any funk!

Hell, when in Rome, I figured. Stripping off, I dived in and joined the throng. Before long, plates of food and beers were lined up along the edge of the pool. This was the kind of last-night revelry I could get used to.

Not for the first time, it occurred to me that the eco-warrior lifestyle could be productive one if you were a viral young bloke.

In a certain way, it reminded me of life in the army, where men stand shoulder to shoulder with their brothers, working hard and playing hard together but, in the military, the set-up was controlled by daily routine. Here, there was a healthy bond between the activists and, although I had only been exposed to it for a week or so, I could feel the close connection they shared with each other every day.

When I surfaced the following morning there were veggie burgers floating in the pool. The sight of them, and the state of my head, told me the night had been a good one.

More food was grilling away – so much for the supplies all being stolen – and it was soon time for a lengthy de-brief to go over with the activists what they could take away from the trip.

Once that was over, we had to pack our things and prepare for the trip back to Manaus. Before we left, however, I felt it was time for some retaliation. I snuck around the back to where the security team's vehicles were and let down their tyres – at least two of each of every car. As we were leaving the Farm, we could see them all standing there scratching their heads, wondering how they'd get out of there. I just waved and, laughing, gave them the one-finger salute. That'll teach them to take me prisoner and subject me to water torture.

Back at the warehouse, the locals were cleaning the kit and getting the vehicles sorted so it was a bit of a down day for us. I was thinking of all the notes I had to write up for SB when Dan, the Scot in charge of logistics, approached me.

'Fancy a wee spin on the RIB?' he said, adding, with a conspiratorial glint in his eye, 'You deserve to unwind a little. Plus, you've yet to sample the delights of Manaus.'

The fast RIB (Rigid Inflatable Boat) was a must for a group like Greenpeace, to patrol the region's mighty rivers. We took to the water but headed for the Rio Negro, the largest blackwater river in the world. Its name literally means black river and it wasn't hard to see why. Humic acid, caused by the incomplete breakdown of phenol-containing plant life gives the water an inky appearance that makes it look like coffee. We swept down to where the river meets the Amazon, where a quirk of nature takes place. Although the two rivers converge their waters remain separate so you can see the black of the Negro alongside the silt brown of the Amazon. As we cut our way through the water, another of nature's wonders was revealed to me – two pink dolphins surfaced by the side of the RIB. The Amazon River dolphin – to give the animal its proper name – is the subject of folklore around those parts. Legend has it that the distinctive pink mammals come out of the river at night, seduce the local women and return to their animal form before morning. Some doubt they even exist but seeing their salmon-coloured flesh close up I can vouch that they are real and truly have a mythical quality about them. It is a sight I will never forget.

While the natural world was mesmerising, we had reached the point in our expedition when we needed refreshment. Dan knew the perfect place – a pontoon bar floating smack bang in the middle of the river Negro. Dan moored alongside and off we hopped to enjoy a cool few beers as the sun went down over the jungle of the Amazon.

When darkness fell, we returned the RIB, went back to the office and met up with two other guys who were up for a night out. We ended up in a bar that seemed respectable enough but after a certain hour transformed into a den of iniquity. It was fascinating to behold. It was as if the clientele knew what was happening. Those who wanted to stay did, those who thought better of it left. Even some of the staff disappeared. In their place were provocatively dressed women who made it perfectly clear what services they were offering and I spent the rest of the evening trying to bat away their advances.

The following night, I had the opportunity to get my notes together from the trip to the Farm. Since I'd been away, my bag hadn't been disturbed and I was confident my participation in the exercise had raised no suspicions whatsoever. I still had a week in the office – plenty of time to observe other goings-on – but I was sure the information I'd gathered so far would curry favour with my handlers. In fact, as I sat on my bunk, I thought if that fucking lot in London don't appreciate my efforts I'll be seriously kicking some arses big-time when I get home! At no stage was I ever of the opinion of being compromised. I had fitted the role perfectly. I was getting off on this intelligence game big time and I felt I had reached my calling at long last.

The remaining days were spent refreshing training manuals on how to lose surveillance, specialist first-aid, and surveillance/protection work. At quieter moments, I sat down with Alison and discussed future projects. Her mind was constantly working, thinking of opportunities and ways to best serve the organisation. We chatted about possible openings for me. She mentioned that the *Rainbow Warrior*, the flagship sunk by the French, was currently in Rotterdam about to go on a tour of duty. She asked if I could help with a pre-deployment security survey. You bet I could.

I sounded her out about helping out their UK office. We touched on some opportunities there. I wasn't to know it then but there was a distinct lack of communication between the international body and its UK office. That was something I would be able to exploit in the coming years.

When the time came to leave, I bade a fond farewell to Alison, Roberto and the rest of the team. They were a good committed bunch and I felt we'd served each other well. I'd given them the benefit of my expertise in areas they hadn't been able to access before, while they'd provided me with a wealth of information.

Dan took me to the airport and, as I boarded my flight, I was tired but happy with my achievements, knowing that doors in Greenpeace UK could soon be opening and with them the promise of more undercover work.

Arriving home, I contacted Terry almost immediately.

'How did it go with the tree-huggers?' he said. 'You gone native yet? Got leaves growing out your arse?'

'Very funny,' I said. 'I don't think you'll be disappointed.

But, look, can I have a week before I get my report to you? I need a couple of days to sort my head out and then I'll get it to you. Once you've had a chance to look through it, we can meet up then to discuss, yeah?'

'Sure, no problem,' he said. 'Next week is fine.'

The compilation of my report took longer than I anticipated. When I went through everything, I'd gleaned the level of intelligence I had to pass on amazed me. Just over a week later, Terry rang to set up a meeting. They'd booked a room at the Novotel at Tower Hill again. When I got there, he was joined by Martin Wilson. They had big smiles on their faces.

'Good work, mate,' Martin said, beaming. 'Very thorough.'

They seemed delighted with everything I'd provided – the identification of the main players, the training methods, the vehicles they used, their protocol, the set-up in Manaus and the etiquette among activists.

'It's impressive,' said Terry. 'It's the first time we've had someone in there.'

When we'd been through the report, I detailed the more colourful elements I'd left out of the written document. They seemed particularly taken with the detail about the communal showers, the skinny-dipping and the sex bar.

'Sounds like you could have done a fair bit of damage out there Ross, old boy,' Wilson said, 'if you'd been that way inclined of course.'

I just nodded and smiled.

'So,' said Terry, 'what's next? Think you can carry this on?'

'No doubt about it,' I said. Since I'd arrived back in the UK, Dan had already been in touch offering to set up an introduction with the chiefs at their UK HQ.

'Great,' said Martin. 'Keep going, then.'

The business with SB was concluded with the small matter of my reward for the information gathered. My cash payment from them was double the payment I received from Greenpeace for assisting with their training. I was happy. If this kept up, the trade in information might be lucrative after all.

SB left me in no doubt about the importance they placed on having someone inside Greenpeace UK. The group had been proving themselves a thorn in the side of the government and big industry in recent years.

Protests at power stations, on board naval warships, oil rigs and at GM crop sites were damaging the reputation of Prime Minister Tony Blair's government, an administration that had once prided itself on its green policies. The resulting publicity from the stunts seemed to have galvanised the UK green movement and the authorities were keen to avoid any future embarrassments. There was the added real concern that the more daring the stunts became the greater the chance that someone could get hurt – something the police and the government were eager to avoid at all costs.

The contact Dan gave me at Greenpeace UK was Steve Packer. The name meant nothing to me but, after I'd done a little research, I realised he was Greenpeace UK's very own action man on many campaigns. He was the real deal, as far as Greenpeace – and probably SB – were concerned.

Steve invited me to their offices in Islington to have a chat. Like the set-up in Brazil, Greenpeace went about their business in London with the same low profile. The group's presence in the area is well known but there's an element of discretion about the premises. The activists don't ram their cause down people's throats.

Once inside, however, it was a different story.

As I entered the building, it was like walking into a different world. Everything was on message, even more so than I witnessed in Brazil. The milk was organic, the toilet paper was recycled and even the beer was organic. Any perceptions the general public might have had about eco-warriors were borne out here.

An efficient reception area led through to a large open-plan office space. Through the back was a dining room and beyond that a garden that led to a warehouse. What was stored in there I wasn't going to be told on this first introductory meeting. The secrecy only made me more intrigued to find out. I was determined to make it my mission to find out everything there was to know about this nerve centre to their whole operation.

My first task, though, was to gain the trust and confidence of their senior team. Steve was the head of the action unit – the wing responsible for all the high-profile stunts. He introduced me to Gemma Davis, the actions director and Harry Taylor, another member of the unit. They were all in their 30s, enthusiastic and committed, as you would expect. Steve was wiry, like a long-distance runner, but clearly possessed a sharp mind and looked like he would be ready to scale a power station at a moment's notice. Gemma was pleasant and friendly and I could almost see her as the public face of the organisation. Articulate and intelligent, I had the sense she was a rising star within the group. I detected Harry Taylor might require a bit more work. I got the sense he was suspicious of newcomers. I might have been paranoid but I got the impression I would need to be careful around him.

Over a cup of tea, I briefed them about my connections to Greenpeace International and my exploits in Brazil. I felt I had their attention and that was good. From their questions, I could see that they saw me as a convert to the cause. My connections with Alison and Dan counted for a great deal and there and then they agreed that I could help train their activists in covert techniques.

The irony that I – someone intent on spying on them – was the one to be invited in to teach them how to spot people like me was something not lost on me. I felt like a fox in the hen house, advising the chickens on security.

The integral role was going to be on a consultancy basis and I could expect to receive a daily rate for my efforts. This suited me fine, especially I was going to be working with the action group – the sharp end. It was exactly what my SB handlers were looking for. I had to gather intelligence on their strengths, identify key players and organisers and, above all, give early warning of anything that would embarrass the UK government.

Once clear of the offices, I called Terry and gave them a situation report as to how it went, which they were very pleased with. At last, they would have someone very close to the nerve centre of one of the UK's largest activist groups and one that caused many headaches with their antics within government circles.

The next two months were spent teaching Steve and his team various skills – many of which I'd educated the people in Brazil – such as surveillance, defensive driving and threat assessments.

It didn't take me long to unlock the secrets of the warehouse. I was referred to Robert, the warehouse manager, who would help me out with the equipment I needed to conduct my courses. He was a likeable guy, happy to help, and he reminded me of Q, the famous quartermaster who provided James Bond with all his gadgets. Like Q, he had a staggering range of equipment at his disposal and the warehouse he managed was like a training centre in its own right. Big enough to hold several RIBs or Rigid Inflatable Boats, it had girders across the ceiling from which activists could learn basic climbing and abseiling techniques.

Robert built models to help teach surveillance techniques and could always lay his hands on the most obscure gear. It was a hugely impressive set-up and one that I could imagine SB didn't have the faintest idea about.

Outside the back of the warehouse was an imposing black exit gate, with a discreet black mailbox on it. I discovered that, while standard Greenpeace mail arrived at the front, this mailbox was registered to a company that at first glance had no connection to Greenpeace. It was only when you dug a little deeper that you discovered Steve and Gemma were listed as directors. Essentially, it was a drop for covert post. All the legitimate stuff went through the front. All the sensitive correspondence went through the back.

It was an interesting office to observe. The Greenpeace UK HQ was an impressive building, referred to as the Boiler House by some. They had about 60 full-time workers and all of them were constantly busy, researching and updating Greenpeace's position on the organisation's core issues – greenhouse gases, tuna fishing, fossil fuels, nuclear dumping etc. These topics of concern might not always generate newspaper headlines but that didn't mean they were off the agenda. They were always under review and being worked on every day. An action plan might take an hour to execute but it would have been meticulously planned for months. They have dedicated research desks and constantly re-evaluated their priorities and where best to utilise their resources. It was very fluid but very well organised. There was always the feeling they were up to something which made it frustrating for me because I knew I wasn't yet privy to the most classified information.

The training commitments with Greenpeace UK extended to several months. Sadly, my workload in Islington was taking up so much time that I had no opportunity to go to Rotterdam, to carry out the security survey on the *Rainbow Warrior*. That was a regret, but things were taking off so well at home that I didn't see the need to push things with Greenpeace International any more.

Still, I kept in contact with Alison. She travelled to London before stopping off on her way to the organisation's international HQ in Amsterdam and we met for a drink to catch up. She was pleased my association with the UK team was growing and I felt happy that my links with the international team were still strong.

I hoped for a chance to break into the inner circle in Islington, but I knew I had to bide my time for the right opportunity. If I tried to force the issue, there was a danger it could arouse suspicion. I knew, though, that if I wanted to get wind of any future stunts, I'd have to gain the complete trust of Steve and Gemma. They seemed to disseminate information on a need-to-know basis.

During this period, I was becoming increasingly wary of

Harry. My initial suspicions were proving correct. I didn't get the impression he was on to me, but he gave the impression of knowing everything that was going on. I'd met some impressive characters since my involvement with Greenpeace began, but this was the first time I thought someone might cause me dangerous problems. He was one person I would have to watch like a hawk.

In the months after my training had finished with Greenpeace UK, I endeavoured to keep my hand in with the organisation. I wanted to make myself available, advise them on any courses of action they opted to take and generally assist them in any way I could.

By autumn 2005 – a year after I'd returned from Brazil – my connections were strong and SB were satisfied with the way things were going. There had been little in the way of high-profile activity and they seemed relaxed that they were in a good position should things change.

I wasn't sure I shared their confidence. I was hungry for some action and wanted a sign that I could break into the action unit.

As it was, I didn't have long to wait. In early November that year, I took a call. It was Gemma. After some initial pleasantries, she got to the point.

'We're planning something that's going to need some extra volunteers,' she said. 'And we need drivers with a Light Goods Vehicle licence.'

Bingo, I thought.

I was in.

CHAPTER 8

THE SOOTY SHOW

I emerged from Aldgate Tube station and made the call.

'Proceed towards Fenchurch Street,' came the curt response. It was Terry but he was in business mode.

'Do a loop of the square in front of the station, then down the lane next to the pub, turn left, first right, first left. We'll have you by then and we'll know if you've been followed or not. When you get there call again.'

'Roger, that,' I said.

New development called for new rules, clearly. Whenever I'd met SB before, there had always been some token anti-surveillance methods employed. I'd only get the location at the last minute and I'd always put into practice my own methodology. Ever since I'd been in touch about Greenpeace's latest action, however, it had moved to a new level.

I did as I was told and made the circuit, pausing to gaze intently into a window and stopping at a cash machine with no intention of withdrawing money. Simple tactics like this frustrated anyone following closely because it forced them to act. The easiest targets are those who blithely proceed to their destination without deviation or hesitation. Then they'll lead you right to where you want to be.

I clocked who I thought was the SB stooge. You'd like to think they used their top guys for jobs like this but invariably it was the FNG – the fucking new guy. You'd also think they'd be able to blend in with their surroundings, but this geezer, in his standard-issue cop plainclothes suit and overcoat, might as well have been looking through a copy of *The Times* with eye holes cut out, he was that conspicuous.

I got to the road in question and figured we must be meeting at the Novotel again – it seemed to be their favourite hang-out. Still, I'd let them have their fun. Called again.

'OK, you're clear,' said Terry. 'Proceed to the Novotel. We've a suite under the name Steele.'

'Righto,' I said.

No Sapphire then, I mused. Shame.

What were they like? Countersurveillance was always good practice in situations like this but I did feel it was compromised slightly by frequently choosing the same place to meet. Nevertheless, I made my way to the suite and found Terry and Martin there. Ordinarily, our meetings would follow the same pattern. I'd brief them of the situation and they'd take their sweet time in getting back to me. This time, however, it had to change. Since I'd contacted them about the latest operation, speed was of the essence. I was receiving nuggets of information all the time. We needed to work out a plan.

Gemma's call had been the one I'd been waiting for. I could never have imagined that it would be my skill as a lorry driver that would unlock the door but in this instance it was invaluable.

'We're planning a DNVA on a major target. It will be extremely high-profile and should have a huge impact,' she had told me.

'I'm all ears,' I said. DNVA was direct non-violent action. Just the kind of protest I wanted to be part of.

'We're going to dump 30 tonnes of coal at a location in central London in protest at Tony Blair's retreat on fossil fuels.'

'Sounds great,' I said. 'Where are we doing it?'

'Does that mean you're in? You won't know the location until the last minute. We don't want anything leaking out.'

'Count me in,' I said.

'Can you drive one of the trucks?'

'Sure. I'll do whatever I can.'

'Great,' Gemma said. 'You'll be getting instructions nearer the time.'

Since then, I knew the dump was happening at 7.30 a.m. on Monday, 14 November. The exact location was still a secret. The operation was codenamed 'The Sooty Show'.

'Nice name,' said Terry. 'So, what are your thoughts on the location?'

'Can only be one of about four,' I said. 'My hunch is that it will either be the House of Commons or 10 Downing Street, or perhaps Westminster Abbey or Buckingham Palace, for the number of tourists that will be there. Big photo opportunity.'

They both nodded.

'When will you know?' Martin said.

'When I pick up the truck,' I said.

'Well, when you pick up the truck, let us know,' Martin said.

I was beginning to get agitated.

'There's a code of conduct on these jobs,' I said. 'They've already said "no phones". What if I can't get a message to you?'

The two SB officers looked at each other.

'And what if I get arrested? I take it you guys will bail me out.'

They exchanged looks again. I had a nauseous feeling in my stomach.

'Best not to let it get to that stage,' Martin said. 'Arrested, I mean. It's not impossible to sort it all out after the event, but it's a ball-ache, to be honest. Better to extract yourself before it gets to that. Think you can do that?'

'If I can get the location to you in advance, it shouldn't be a problem. You'll be able to stop it before it happens, then won't you?'

'Not necessarily,' Martin said. 'Sometimes it's better to let them get on with it. Let the local lids handle it.'

He was meaning the uniformed cops – known as lids because of their distinctive helmets. I was slightly apprehensive about the advice regarding the arrests. This was where my role was tricky. How do I prove to Greenpeace I'm a willing participant but stop short of taking a direct role so I could avoid being arrested? It was impossible to predict what would happen. I just had to keep my wits about me and hope that an opportunity presented itself.

The dump was now less than a week away. Gemma had

told me to expect more communication through the post. It duly arrived on Friday, three days before the operation.

Titled 'The Sooty Show', it gave us details of a hostel where we had to meet on Sunday evening at 6 p.m. and went on:

'Do not mention Greenpeace on your arrival.

'Please ensure that you have had some food before you arrive. An evening meal will be provided.

'The event will take place on the morning of Monday, 14 November, and we hope that you will be able to return home in the evening, but this obviously depends on how things unfold.'

It sounded ominous and was an obvious reference to potential arrests. In some ways reminiscent of a Scout camp notification, the letter went on:

'Please bring with you: Things for an overnight stay (you will not need a sleeping bag/mat), a book, good boots, layered clothing.

'Please do not bring: a car, a mobile phone, anything which is marked as Greenpeace, e.g. bags, clothing, literature.'

Time was now of the essence. I tried to kick-start SB into a more definitive response. We urgently needed a more concrete plan in my opinion. They seemed to be leaving too much to chance. I relayed the contents of the letter to Terry. Fairly swiftly, I got a response, stating they wanted to meet me at Stansted Airport on the Sunday morning. Now they were really pushing their luck and I still had no idea of the target.

I had to hope by then I'd have some idea, or the means to pass the information on to them. I was running of time to even start worrying about it.

The following day, the other drivers and I convened at the Islington office for further instructions. We were to be given privileged information because we needed to get the trucks in position. It was time for the coal run. Gemma and Steve explained that we were to be driven in a truck to Oxfordshire, where we'd pick up the lorries and then head to collect the coal.

'From there, you'll take the lorries to the Farm,' said Steve, 'where they'll stay until we depart on Monday morning.'

What was this? The Farm? I'd never heard anyone within Greenpeace refer to a place out of London before. It reminded me of the place in Brazil, but something told me this was much different. For a start, it sounded like their own depot, not some camp they were having the use of.

I left my car at Islington and joined the rest of the driving team in the truck to Oxfordshire. We picked up the lorries as planned at a weighbridge. The empty lorries were weighed. I volunteered to look after the hire-agreement paperwork and gleefully stuffed the documents into my pocket. Contained in there were the registration numbers and specifications of both vehicles – reasonably helpful to SB, I thought.

I was driving a seven-and-a-half-tonner. We had another one the same size there waiting for us as well. There was talk of another lorry, a huge 20-tonne HGV, but it was being organised outwith our little satellite mission and would meet us at the Farm. With the weights checked off, we went again in convoy to a very remote farm in Bicester, where both trucks were loaded to the limit of seven and a half tonnes of coal. With our loads, we returned to the weigh-station and both vehicles passed the weight check of seven and a half tonnes. All set, it was time to drive, in a small convoy, down to Hertfordshire and to this mysterious Farm. It was pitch-black by the time we got there and, because I was following another driver, it was tricky to work out exactly where I was. I tried to make a note of landmarks we passed, but it proved impossible to pin down the precise location. Every building, track and road looked the same to me, so I just adopted the sheep mentality and followed behind like everyone else.

Eventually, we stopped, and one of the other drivers, Kevin, came over to us and said we were close now but had to turn the truck lights off on the approach. It was all very cloak-and-dagger. I followed the convoy and drove slowly in to an opening. I stopped the truck just over the edge of the gravel driveway. Suddenly, there was a commotion among the guys around the truck in front. It turned out this wasn't the Farm. It was so secret even Greenpeace workers couldn't find it!

Instead, we'd come into some rich private estate. The driver of the other truck couldn't manoeuvre his way out so asked me to move mine over. I edged over a little and this is where the fun began. As I slipped into low gears, the wheels spun off the gravel track and I felt the back end suddenly embed itself in the perfectly laid lawn. I tried to go forward and then backward, but to no avail. The wheels had repositioned themselves and my truck was firmly stuck in the middle of a lawn. Even in the darkness, I could see it was a garden befitting Hampton Court Palace.

I couldn't believe it. Don't tell me we won't be able to complete the mission as planned because I've got the bloody lorry stuck.

With seven and a half tonnes of coal onboard, I was going nowhere fast. We spent more than 90 minutes trying to free the truck with coal, gravel and wood under the wheels, but nothing would shift it at all. In fact, the load sank my truck even deeper and the back of the truck was now only three and a half feet from touching the grass itself.

The only thing in our favour was that the owner of this lovely establishment was out for the night and would not see the new garden and churned up lawn until the next morning.

Eventually, Kevin phoned Steve and told him the bad news. The remaining truck located the correct farm and was hidden undercover. The crew then came back to pick me up and head back to London. I got a lift back to civilisation and made arrangements to get home. There, I copied the paperwork to pass to SB in the morning. I was frustrated that I was no further forward to knowing anything about the elusive Farm, but felt sure I'd get a second chance that night, when it came to pick up the lorries.

I kept my appointment with Terry and Martin and, using another car, headed over to meet them at a hotel near Stansted Airport. On my way there, I tried to place my role in all of this. If all went according to Greenpeace's plan, I'd be driving a truck into the heart of London to dump coal outside a famous landmark, no doubt causing disruption and creating one hell of a publicity coup. It didn't seem real, somehow. It might have been a different location, but the same rules applied. SB put me through the same counter-surveillance ritual before I was considered clear, and signalled to the hotel. Given how early it was, I took advantage of their offer of breakfast and tucked into a full fry-up.

It took them a few minutes to compose themselves once I'd told them about the previous night's farce.

'Nice one, Ross,' Terry said, laughing. 'You're meant to be saving the planet and there you are tearing up some poor bugger's lawn. You'll be lucky if they take you back.'

'Yeah, I know,' I said, trying to see the funny side. 'Good thing I'm the only person who can drive the bloody thing.'

That much was true. Even if Greenpeace were miffed at the cock-up, they'd never find a replacement driver at this late stage. Plus, I consoled myself, it was hardly my fault if I'm led to the wrong bloody farm. The officers were very intrigued at the presence of the Farm and vowed to send a helicopter up to find it if I could provide a more accurate location.

We chatted for an hour, but one thing I needed to clear up before our meeting was over was the subject of my immunity from prosecution. It was a complicated situation because immunity can't be granted for the whole of London for a specific time. They needed to know specifics. On this occasion, however, they agreed it was safer to grant it to me for the locations we discussed. If it ended up that we were heading somewhere else, it was going to be a major problem.

I signed the declaration that meant I'd be considered as an innocent individual rather than an operative. So long as I did not act as an agent provocateur or seriously break the rules, I would be fine. We all left fairly satisfied. I had my protection and they had everything bar the target. They could start alerting the relevant authorities should they see fit.

Back home, I packed my kit and tried to get into

character for my debut performance as a crusty tree-hugging protester. I had half a beard growing, I matted my hair down, stuck in an earring and dug out some dowdy old clothes. There, I thought, as I admired myself in the mirror, that should pass as an eco-warrior.

At 4.45 p.m., I strode into the hostel where we had been advised to meet. Many of the volunteers were there already and the scene resembled the great gunpowder plot. Everyone was sitting on the floor looking at maps and discussing the filming of the job that would be flashed out to the press and TV stations once the hit was made. I didn't recognise any of them and many looked at me in shock when I entered. I explained I was merely a driver looking for a bunk. Fortunately, one of the Islington staff twigged who I was and welcomed me into the fold. That seemed to do the trick. The jumpy ones breathed out and relaxed their sphincters.

At 6 p.m. sharp, everyone was called downstairs for the final briefing. People handed in mobile phones, watches and any Greenpeace-branded items, so they could be transported to Islington and handed back at the end of the day tomorrow. I kept my phone on me. I could ill afford to lose my only contact with SB.

With all blinds pulled down and doors closed and guarded, a team of retained solicitors began a legal briefing on the implications of the action, covering the help-lines to call in case of emergency and a word of warning that the police we would encounter would most likely be heavily armed given the nature of our target. Before the main briefing began – and the location of the coal dump revealed – everyone was given a last chance to bail out. No one did.

It was then time for the main event. Steve, a veteran of a similar and very successful stunt in Washington, did the honours.

'Our target, people, is 10 Downing Street,' he said. As an excited buzz swept the room, he continued: 'We aim to block all three exits to Number 10 with over 30 tonnes of coal. One lorry will cover the rear, the other will take the side, while the HGV will take out the main entrance off Whitehall. It's going to be huge, people.'

Some people were whooping. The group certainly agreed with the choice of target.

My first reaction was elation that I had guessed correctly. My second was how the fuck do I get this information to SB, without being compromised?

'Once the coal's in place, we'll sit back and wait for the shit to hit the proverbial,' Steve continued. 'It will be a significant victory if Blair's diary is disrupted and he can't even leave for Parliament.'

I doubted this part of his plan would come to pass. With SB fully aware of the operation, if not the specific target, and the Diplomatic Protection Group probably now informed, they'd be waiting for them. I hope you have a Plan B, I thought to myself.

The briefing concluded with a run-through for the volunteers of the rendezvous point, which was to be at Waterloo Place. It seemed a bit too close for comfort for my liking but they're the ones calling the shots I thought. They must know what they're doing.

As soon as the meeting was over, the other drivers and me had time for a quick meal and then it was time to leave for the Farm. Once again, it was dark by the time we left the lights of the M11 but I was prepared this time and kept a mental map of our turnings and landmarks.

My vantage point in the back of the van wasn't ideal, but I managed to spy a pub not far from the motorway junction. Closing my eyes, I used the rolling of the vehicle to ascertain which direction we were going and counted in seconds between each turning to give me some sense of distance.

Finally, I could tell by the way the van was slowing that we'd reached the entrance to the Farm. I just hoped we had the right one this time. I'd already heard from Gemma earlier that my lorry had been extracted from the lawn by two tractors and had been delivered as planned, albeit sometime later than expected. She mentioned that Greenpeace would have to foot the bill to repair the disgruntled bloke's lawn. Oops!

When I emerged from the van, I couldn't believe my eyes. What was this place? The van had parked on a large concrete hardstanding that was effectively a huge farmyard. Immediately facing me was a large Dutch barn. Hanging from the roof were massive missiles. I assumed they weren't real but to see them hanging there, lit up by a portable floodlight while everything around us was cloaked in darkness, was quite an image. Next to the missiles were RIBs and other boats. Clearly, this was Greenpeace's holding area – a depot for all the vehicles they'd need for land and water assaults. It was mightily impressive. I was also amazed they'd been able to keep it secret.

We didn't have long to prepare the trucks for the following morning. Further along from the missiles were more covered barns, big enough to house the lorries. I recognised the two we'd delivered yesterday but dwarfing them alongside was the massive HGV, looking menacing in the pitch-black. Like the others, it was brimming with coal, all 20 tonnes of it.

Within seconds, everyone was busy taping Greenpeace signs to the sides of all the vehicles but then completely sheeting the lorries up so no one would see the cargo or the carrier until the last minute. That way, they hoped, they might evade the attention of the police until they got to Downing Street.

By the time we'd finished, it was 1 a.m. The work completed, we retired to a nearby Travelodge for a couple of hours' kip before it was time to hit the road.

My career as an eco-warrior was about to begin.

CHAPTER 9

TARGETING NUMBER 10

One text message. That was what it was hanging on now.

When the destination had finally been revealed, I had fidgeted in my pocket. I couldn't let anyone see what I was doing. I'd worked out the buttons to press to send a text message to Terry.

I only sent one digit – the number '2'. It was what we agreed. That should have been enough to tell them Downing Street was the target. Number '1' had been the House of Commons, '3' Westminster Abbey and '4' Buckingham Palace. They had the rest of the details:7.30 a.m., 14 November, three lorries, three locations.

I wondered whether I needed to stress that each of the lorries would take an exit. Would they work that out? What if they prepared for a main-gate assault and were left red-faced when the other exits were ambushed. Surely, they'd be prepared for any eventuality. It was after 1 am when I finally had some time on my own in the Travelodge. I was tempted to call, send another text to confirm.

Yet, Terry had texted back his confirmation that he'd got and understood the message. Surely, that was enough. I couldn't lay everything on for them, could I? They were big boys, they had to think for themselves at some point.

Even though I was dog-tired, I tossed and turned. I willed my body to sleep but the adrenalin was getting the better of me. What were these? Last-minute nerves? Guilt? Was I bothered I was betraying my new-found colleagues? Seeing the elation on their faces was something I hadn't prepared for. They were clearly up for this. For some of the activists and volunteers who had joined in the last year or so, this was the pinnacle of their involvement, their reason for joining the cause. To stick it to the heart of government and make a political point was why some of them got out of bed in the morning. And little did they know that a spy in their midst was plotting to royally fuck it up for them.

No, I told myself. It's your duty to inform the authorities. Greenpeace might mean well but, without prior warning, all hell could break loose when you pull a stunt in front of armed police. The ideal scenario for me would be if the coppers let them have their five minutes of fame but the forewarning means that in no way will the PM be disrupted or compromised. Not to mention me. We can all win out of this, I told myself. It will all work out fine.

It was with these thoughts running through my mind that the buzz finally subsided and I drifted off to sleep.

It was one of those nights when I felt like I'd been in the deepest slumber as the alarm rudely awakened me at 4 a.m. However, it was barely two hours later.

In half an hour, we were back at the farm. In the freezing cold we had a final briefing on the route plan. We were to go straight down the M11, through Hackney, through the City and over to Pall Mall and down to Waterloo Place. We were all to rendezvous with the volunteers there at 6 a.m.

The more I thought about the rendezvous point, the more I thought it was a bonkers idea. It's a small road off Pall Mall but it's where the Foreign Secretary's house is, so is therefore heavily policed. At the end of the street are some steps that lead to the Mall. A more conspicuous location for three huge lorries you couldn't have hoped to pick.

The only vehicle that wasn't going to meet up with the others was the huge HGV. That was making its own way to Downing Street via Whitehall.

We had a specific route to avoid cameras picking us up. The weakest link could be the route being wrong. It could have proved problematic but common sense prevailed and I arrived at the rendezvous in good time. Despite the bungling, the minibuses soon arrived at Waterloo Place with the activists, who were to help unload the coal at the various exits. We were nearly at the point of execution but I have to say everyone was calm and focused, myself included.

Harry Taylor came over to my truck and told us to put our high-visibility vests on, take the coverings off the vehicles and make them ready for the dump. With three people, all wearing thick winter coats, in the cab, it was impossible for us to manoeuvre, so we hopped out, stripped the vehicle covers off, and put the vests on. Taylor went mad.

'You fucking idiots,' he screamed. 'Now everyone can see your bloody Greenpeace vests.'

I didn't have the heart to point out that he was standing next to two large lorries with GREENPEACE emblazoned down the side, so the time for discretion had passed somewhat. Instead, I just let him have his rant. He was obviously stressed.

Taylor calmed down and told me to get rid of the maps we'd been using to bring us here.

'Shove them in that post box over there,' he said, motioning to a pillar box at the end of the street. This was also a bonkers suggestion.

'The first thing a postie will do on seeing marked maps in a pillar box a stone's throw from Buckingham Palace and the Foreign Secretary's house will be to call the police,' I said to my crew-mate. 'Then see how long it takes them to prove a conspiracy from the fingerprints all over them.'

At least I didn't have to worry about breaking any laws so again I did as I was told and posted the maps.

As the whole operation threatened to implode, I was reminded of the old army saying: 'SNAFU!' – 'situation normal all fucked up'.

At 7 a.m., it was time to put the plan into action. We mounted up and were given the signal to move off. I was behind Taylor's vehicle, with the activists' minibuses behind us. We turned left and went past Clarence House, towards the Mall. Just then, a copper on foot patrol walked towards the convoy. I felt certain we'd be stopped and the whole operation foiled before it began. Incredibly, however, he simply glanced in our direction, thought nothing of two big lorries brimming over with coal and carried on his way. This was swiftly turning into a farce.

The lights turned green, and we turned left down the Mall and then right into Horse Guards' Road. Taylor started to speed up, so I hung back and let him go. Upon reaching the rear entrance of Downing Street, he swung out across the road and slammed into reverse. The coppers on the rear gate were at a loss and one came running out to stop him reversing. Ignoring the officer's pleas to stop, Taylor backed it up at high speed.

I casually swerved around Taylor's vehicle and, without fuss, drew up close to King Charles Street to allow the activists to carry the coal off my truck and run with it to the side entrance to Downing Street. The two-man crew with me jumped out and started handing sacks of coal off the back of my truck to the waiting volunteers. I merely sat there watching the whole scenario unfold.

In my rear- view mirror,, I could see that Taylor's tipper hadn't yet deposited its coal. I later discovered a volunteer, upon coming into contact with a very pissed-off copper, had lost his bottle. Taylor had then jumped out of the cab and kicked the release flap free, dumping the coal right across the exit way. The poor copper did not know whether to bollock Taylor for his sheer brass neck or try to stop the deluge of coal spilling onto the street. Apart from the valiant efforts of the guards on the gate, there was no sign of London's finest anywhere.

I couldn't work out if this was part of a strategy or simply incompetence on behalf of the cops. A full eight minutes had passed since we arrived at the home of the PM before I heard the sirens of the Diplomatic Branch arriving. Even then, it was only two motorbikes and one car. Hardly the cavalry. By then, it was too late. My truck was empty and so too was Taylor's. Seven minutes after that, two Territorial Support Group (TSG) vans arrived and parked in front of my truck.

I wound the window down, and the sergeant just told me to move on without delay, which I tried to do, but two of my crew were still on the back and would have been injured had I done so. Eventually, another PC came over and dutifully took my details. He name-checked me. I'm not sure what came up but he then tried to discreetly talk to me at one side but I was having none of it. Safe in the knowledge that I had immunity and confident that this would all end with a minimum of fuss, I refused to play ball.

Eventually, we were free to go with nothing more than a good telling-off – not that it mattered to me!

The plan was to head back to the Farm. I drove through central London but, as I approached some traffic lights in Camden, I saw a TSG van pull out of a side turning and follow me. The lights were at amber. Suspecting a police tail – and being right on the stop line – I carried on through. If my suspicions were correct, I'd pull the police van through with me. Sure enough, he passed through the red. He was clearly following us.

For the next hour, I dragged them through all of London's traffic. The last thing I wanted to do was return to the Farm with a police van behind me. Never mind that I'd been trying to give SB the exact location so they could have a snoop around! I didn't want to lead the cops to it this way. Besides, to hold my credibility, I could not be seen helping the police in any way. I pulled over after an hour and looked at a map. The TSG van drew up next to my window. The copper in the front asked, in a sarcastic manner, 'You lost?'

'Er, yes, I think I might be,' I said. 'Don't you, officer?'

He didn't have a sense of humour.

'Just keep moving, get out of town and stay away, or you'll be nicked. Understood?'

We drove out of the city unmolested and, with the help of my two crewmates, found the Farm with slightly less hassle than I had on that first night. As we pulled in, I saw that by the front of the main farmhouse were several large white flag stones. Surely they would be spotted from the air.

It was only when we met up with other Greenpeace guys that we discovered what had happened to the rest of the crews. The HGV didn't reach its target. Its size meant it breached new regulations on vehicles permitted into the city centre due to fuel emissions. An eagle-eyed traffic cop saw it and pulled it over. That was sheer bad luck, but, actually, it was a major embarrassment for Greenpeace. How can an organisation that prides itself on promoting lower emissions be banned from entering a city because it is polluting the atmosphere? You couldn't make it up. It was a lack of due diligence on their part.

While the rest of us were allowed to leave with no more than a slap on the wrist, Taylor later told me he was convicted and given points on his licence and a fine that was paid by Greenpeace.

The initial reaction among Greenpeace activists seemed to be that the stunt was a success. They got the footage they wanted and the lack of police response seemed to suggest they knew nothing in advance. All that remained to be seen was the coverage they garnered on the TV news later that day and in the newspapers the following day.

Once I was relieved of my duties, I took a call from Terry.

'Great job, mate,' he said. 'Everything went like clockwork.'

'That's good to hear,' I said. 'From the response, I wondered what was going on.'

'Everyone who needed to know did,' he added. 'Including the PM.'

'Really?' I said. 'How so?'

'His security advisers told him the night before that a covert op was being conducted and he had nothing to worry about. He watched the drama unfold over his breakfast in the morning. His schedule wasn't interrupted in the slightest.'

I was thrilled. It couldn't have gone any better, it seemed.

'Everyone in the Yard is happy,' Terry added.

Terry explained that the Diplomatic Protection Group superintendent was kept informed, but he didn't brief the early shift on what was happening. That was slightly alarming. It meant the response – or lack of it – wasn't based on any prior knowledge. They were just slow off the mark. If anything, the operation – and my part in it – exposed their failings. If Greenpeace had wanted to get away with more they could have. Eight minutes response time is unacceptable when the safety of the Prime Minister is at stake.

Apparently, a couple of units from the public order team were hold up further down the road. They had been told there might be an incident in the morning but they didn't know who was behind it or what it was all about.

The following morning's headlines were devoted to the

stunt. The failure of the main lorry to deliver its load didn't seem to merit a mention. Only a few papers picked up on the quick-thinking copper that foiled Greenpeace. Elsewhere, it was a publicity coup. It made headlines around the world and brought sharp focus on Tony Blair's green credentials, which had been taking a battering since he had swept into power in the 1997 general election. More importantly, the protest put Greenpeace once again at the forefront of people's minds. The organisation, which made its name during its heyday in the 1980s by taking on the whaling fleets and protesting against nuclear waste, had sometimes struggled to stay relevant in this ever-changing world. Here, though, they'd shown they were still capable of influencing the agenda with attention-grabbing stunts.

In the next couple of days, I would go into the offices in Islington for a full run-down of how the top brass gauged how it went. I was satisfied I had done enough to become part of the fold. Pleased with how things had gone, I was looking forward to being involved to a greater extent in all their operations.

Little did the action unit know, however, that, by the time they would see me again, the location of their secret staging post in the middle of the Hertfordshire countryside would be well known to Special Branch. Thanks to my directions, a helicopter had spotted the flagstones and found its location.

They'd won a moral victory today. But, now they had invited a double agent into their inner circle, at what cost would it be to them in the long term?

CHAPTER 10

TRADECRAFT

Being a double agent or a spy can sound glamorous but the reality can be very different. It's a lonely existence, with long periods of inaction punctuated only briefly by moments of activity which are often highly stressful. You don't see that side in James Bond films!

The upside, however, is that it is a life of ever-changing circumstances, where operatives have to live on their wits, constantly thinking of ways to outsmart their quarry. When it all goes well and you complete an operation and everyone's happy it's deeply rewarding. The trouble is, to get to that stage you have to endure a lot of stress and you can be testing yourself emotionally and physically.

It certainly takes a certain type of person to want to be a covert operator. But, with the right training, anyone can turn their hand to it. And, inside the depths of espionage at home or abroad, it's essential you have the right tradecraft.

Espionage has been with us since the time of the Romans and as long as humans walk the planet they'll be thinking of ways of deceiving each other. It is not a new type of skill by any means, but one that has been honed over the years to suit the advancement of humans and technology.

So, how do you define tradecraft as practiced in the dark world of spooks and faceless shadows? In essence, it means that any skill that has been learnt and practiced and then applied to a clandestine operation. It can cover everything from verbal deception to computer theft.

My personal definition is that 'tradecraft is a variation of the truth', and that covers a whole multitude of sins.

My initiation into tradecraft was a baptism of fire, when, in the late 1970s, in Northern Ireland, I began what was known as 'sneaky beaky stuff' with the Parachute Regiment in west Belfast. As a lad of just 18 years old, the thought of mixing with terrorists and their sympathisers was as frightening as acknowledging death itself.

When I joined the army, I found that wearing the uniform gave me a sense of security and identity. But when I was ordered to go out in plainclothes, with a 9-mm strapped to my waist, I felt as naked as the day I was born. That feeling of vulnerability normally comes about because of the sudden and forced disassociation with your military identity.

The sneaky stuff I was involved in was not so much deep undercover work as intelligence spotting. Even so, it was a good introduction to the art of tradecraft. The cars were kitted out with covert radios and we were told to dress scruffily to fit in with the environment we were to be in.

My first taste of covert surveillance was to come one Monday in March 1977, at around 5 p.m., when the hustle and bustle was at its height and when it might be easier to spot the masters of the IRA Belfast Brigade.

At a briefing beforehand, we were shown photos of the entire brigade we were targeting, their families and associates and the places they frequented. We were then told to use all available methods to identify the key players and to gather intelligence on any new faces and premises in an area that had not previously been reported on. Being fairly new to this covert stuff, I was paired with a more experienced guy called Keith, a diminutive Geordie with an acid tongue.

During a pre-patrol chat, he explained the necessary SOPs (standard operating procedures) for a job like this.

'Make your moves positive, don't hesitate, look confident but don't open your mouth and reveal your accent,' he said.

He said moving in and out of the base was always precarious as this was when we were most vulnerable to getting bumped and when the nerves were stretched most. Fifteen minutes later, we were muddling our way along the Falls Road in rush-hour traffic, aiming for Mackies foundry, a place that was always alive with IRA sympathisers.

I was dropped off about 500 yards from the factory entrance, to proceed on foot and see if I could identify any suspects. It started to drizzle, which in itself was good cover, as it is not out of place to put your head down or put a hood up, which is exactly what I did. My pulse was racing and I attempted to control my breathing after stepping out of the car as casually as I could, to make my way to the factory exit.

I felt alone and exposed and the fear generated was almost overpowering. I felt a chill to my bones, not from the weather but from sheer nerves.

I walked slowly up the street, until I came to the yard, scanning everything as I went. At the exit, I tried to make myself look inconspicuous by building a roll-up cigarette. This proved harder than it sounds because my hands were shaking so much. As the workers left, I scanned their faces looking for anyone we knew. Keith sat a distance away watching my every move. We'd established a hand signal code. If I broke into a coughing fit with my hand at my mouth, he would know I was in trouble. If I took my gloves off and put them in my left pocket, it would mean there was nothing of interest.

There was nothing to indicate I was compromised but, nevertheless, I felt I had a thousand pairs of eyes on me. I crossed the road and made towards the pre-arranged rendezvous point. Only as I crossed the road did I feel anything like an adrenalin rush. As I walked along, I had to be alert to any possible tails. It meant I had to employ a number of little procedures designed to help you avoid detection. These included mixing in with groups of people and walking in the same direction and speed as them, shuffling from one side of the pavement to the other, integrating as best I could and being nondescript to anyone looking for signs of surveillance or infiltration.

The day passed without incident and we eventually gleaned some snippets of intelligence that fed into the file we were creating on the Belfast Brigade; but I always remember it as my first tentative steps into another world.

The ability to blend in is an art in itself that requires

consideration and forethought. You will always find surveillance teams in dark colours, free of designs or logos that will make you stand out. Surveillance or observation teams will have a complete array of props on hand, usually in the vehicles accompanying them, including reversible and different-coloured jackets, white sticks for blind people, hats, briefcases and umbrellas when in the field, in order to distort and confuse the thoughts of any hostile operator.

Extreme dress codes can work in certain circumstances. For one meeting where I had to discuss a potential Russian threat with MI6 that was taking place in Covent Garden, I adopted long shorts and a garish top, so that I would blend in with the tourists. I even had a Tube map and asked a policeman for directions to confuse any would-be tails.

Foreign-intelligence agencies all recognise the basic tradecraft and generally add their own variations to this. Within the UK, tradecraft is taught mainly at Fort Monkton, an imposing castle-style building near Portsmouth, where MI6 training takes place. It's where agents learn the art of spying. Here, many tricks of the trade are imparted, but not before the test of someone's basic abilities is made. From day one, a candidate's internal strength and resolve are tested and it is during this period that the trainee agent realises the stark reality of what is being asked of him. Despite them knowing it is a training scenario, the amount of intense pressure converts their mind into one of truth and reality of the situation which is set out before them.

Tradecraft candidates will find themselves in very precarious situations. Often, they are given a goal to achieve, say the passport number of a random stranger in a pub. Away from home, away from friends and away from their comfort zones, the agents are armed with only one thing – their own guile.

I know one agent who, upon entering the pub, took his time to survey the area he found, first, to negate any counterintelligence operatives that may have be present and, then, to carefully select his victim. With the pub moderately busy, the decision was to target two females sat at a table together. Next, came the introduction and build-up phase, where he engaged the women in a conversation. He told them he was on a European luxury ship that had docked locally and was out recruiting for staff for the next leg of the voyage sailing into every port in the Caribbean. He needed extra staff for the two-month trip, as some crew had gone sick and, as things were desperate, the pay had been increased ten-fold in order to fill the gap in numbers. It was rather fortunate that unemployment in this area was rife and the ploy worked on the two women.

With alcohol in abundance and tall stories to match, one of the victims was hooked and immediately went home to return with her passport some ten minutes later. She handed over the number quite willingly, especially when he gave her the phone number of a purser to ring to check his story. It was actually support staff at Fort Monkton. He later came clean to her and told her that it was all a ruse for a training exercise but the woman was compensated for her trouble.

It is not unusual to employ this phone technique and it happens on most undercover jobs. A glance into a live-ops room will find telephone booths with brief details as to how the phone should be answered such as a company name etc. Certainly, at New Scotland Yard, there were a small bank of these booths live at most times ready to back the agent up should someone decide to double-check the credentials of an undercover officer or verify some aspect by the target.

The same stringent training regime applies to the National Undercover School at the Metropolitan Police College at Hendon, North London.

The need for in-depth profiling of a candidate prior to being accepted as a police undercover agent is very difficult indeed and will see the candidate undergo many written tests and interviews including one with a retained psychologist. The problem is, the answers given in written tests or verbal interviews are neither right nor wrong and I certainly found that you may answer question number 6 one way but then get asked exactly the same question at number 20 but phrased in a totally reverse way just to assess your train of thought.

Once a potential undercover officer has completed the 'Nut and Gut' tests, as they are called, and walks through the gates at Hendon he leaves behind him his entire identity and life without compromise. 'You are not Ross Slater, you are Bertie Henshaw now, so don't let me or any of the course instructors hear different or you will be binned,' is the helpful advice from the head honcho at the course introduction talk.

One female officer had kept up her new identity all day but during her lunch break was heard by an instructor making a personal call home to check on her child. She was removed from the course. Another officer was required to take a police covert vehicle home for the weekend ready for an exercise on the Monday morning. He'd taken the car to the supermarket when another car collided with his.

Forgetting his new alias, he exchanged his real details. The other driver was an instructor – most likely a plant. The officer was off the course.

It sounds extreme but it's vitally important to instil that fear that your life depends on you sticking to your assumed identity.

In recent times, many campaigners for human rights have questioned what the precise remit of a police undercover officer actually is. When I was in the Met, the job specification for all undercover officers was this:

'At the directions of the Senior Investigating Officer to meet persons who may have a varied criminal background and social standing in order to cultivate acquaintances and gain their confidence by undertaking the required roles for varying scenarios with the object of securing intelligence and the evidence for arrest and conviction of persons involved in criminal activity at all times working within the confines of the law, in particular those affecting agent provocateur and of unfair evidence.

'To be prepared to give evidence of their actions / conduct during an undercover operation.'

To my mind, this still holds good to this day. What is a murky issue is how far the police can establish whether criminal activity is definitely taking place before they launch a covert operation. Otherwise they can be accused of going on a fishing expedition to see what they can unearth.

If I had been a serving undercover officer, would the Met have sent me in to infiltrate Greenpeace? Certainly, the organisation had a long history of carrying out peaceful action to further their aims, whether it be causing a public nuisance or trespassing onto private property or causing disruption to make a political point. Would the Met have been justified sending in an undercover on the back of these protests?

It's debatable. That's maybe why, when I first discussed my role within Greenpeace, SB declined to look a gift horse in the mouth and seized their opportunity.

Without me, the Downing Street incident could have been a major embarrassment for the government. My infiltration of Greenpeace UK had got off to a good start. All I needed to know was, would it last?

CHAPTER 11

HIGH TIMES

'Here you go, mate, have a smoke,' Steve said. It was a measure of how much I'd been accepted by the upper echelons of Greenpeace UK that I was the only outsider invited to their Christmas party in 2005. This was a Christmas Party Greenpeace-style, and it was a bit of an eye-opener. They kept it in-house, which was understandable given the antics that went on. And by in-house, I mean, within the close circle, as well as holding the festivities in the Boiler House. Mostly, only regular staffers were invited. Even though I was by no means a full-time employee – my casual day-rate agreement was still in place – the fact that I was invited showed how much I was now one of them. None of the volunteers – even those who had taken part in the recent protest in Downing Street – were there. The only other people there were the legal advisers who worked on Greenpeace's behalf.

I felt privileged and satisfied that everything was going to plan. Gemma and Steve had been delighted with the way the coal protest had gone. The resulting publicity was better than they hoped for and, at a post-event debriefing session, Steve praised everyone for how well the plan was executed.

'It was obvious they hadn't a clue we were coming,' he told the assembled staff (again no volunteers were present at this meeting). He'd earlier made a point of saying he'd been pleased with my efforts, which dispelled any fears I might have had that Harry Taylor might have made life difficult for me.

Interestingly, at that debrief, Gemma asked the staff if any of the volunteers had given cause for concern. A few of the more experienced hands mentioned some who didn't pull their weight and much was made of the guy who'd bolted from Taylor's truck when he should have been operating the tipper. For an organisation that relied on help from volunteers, they weren't slow about turfing them out if they weren't up to scratch.

For my part, I raised the issue I'd had with Taylor's idea about sticking the used maps into the post box.

'Maybe next time, we should think about taking prepared envelopes to post the maps in,' I said. 'Less chance of us being rumbled that way.'

'Good point, Ross,' said Steve. 'Yes, we should have thought of that.'

Taylor glowered at me. I'm sure, if he had his way, I'd have been out of there with the ropey volunteers. And he must have been even more delighted to see me at the Christmas party.

The festivities had started sedately enough, with some games of pool with Steve, but as the organic beer flowed the atmosphere turned to one not dissimilar from that in the camp in Brazil once the exercise had finished.

That organic booze had nearly made me barf, so that was one reason to stay sober, but I'd already planned not to get too out of it. I wanted to keep my wits about me and observe what was going on.

As the party raged on, it became clear that people were keen to hook up all over the place. I abstained from any funny business but I could see relationships were another area where undercover operatives could and did come unstuck. If you were immersing yourself in a culture and way of life, it would take the will power of a saint to resist all the opportunities that came your way. If you spend your days denying another life that exists outside the role you inhabit, it must be incredibly difficult to stay on the right side of the line. It's where I was determined to remain, however.

When it got past 2 a.m. and the revelry showed no sign of ending, I grabbed a few sleeping bags and got my head down in one of the RIBs in the warehouse. It wasn't the most comfortable night I've ever had in my life but, compared to a hammock and a mosquito net in the jungle, it wasn't bad by Greenpeace standards. I woke at 7 a.m. By the noise upstairs, I could tell the party was still going strong. I got my kit together and snuck out the back and had to scale the fence to make an escape.

A week later, I had my Christmas drinks with the guys from SB. This double-agent life wasn't so bad after all. Theirs was a more traditional affair but there was beer you could drink and sometimes that's enough for a good time. Plus, they came bearing gifts.

'Here you go,' Terry said, handing me an envelope. 'You've earned it.'

I glanced inside. It was a wad of notes. It looked like several thousand.

'Consider it a Christmas bonus,' Martin added, raising a glass.

'Wow, thanks,' I said. I genuinely wasn't expecting another payday from them. The way we had been working had suited me fine. After the Downing Street job, I was well rewarded. SB gave me much more than the couple of shifts I earned from Greenpeace for actually doing the work. The environmentalists didn't believe in overtime so four long days boiled down to nearly nothing. SB, on the other hand, were delighted with the outcome and paid accordingly.

In the intervening period, I had been tipping them off with information unconnected to Greenpeace. I had contacts in Iraq and Afghanistan who tipped me off with any security issues. Like they'd done with Interpol and Greenpeace International, SB were happy to liaise with other agencies because of the kudos it brought them. On these occasions, they passed my info up the food chain to MI6. I was proving valuable to them on more than one level.

While we chatted and the beers kept coming, Terry mentioned a curious footnote to the Downing Street job. SB's inquiries about the Farm had led them to a startling discovery. The property in Hertfordshire belonged to a former policeman. His name was on the deeds. If SB had known how close the police actually was to the nerve centre of the environmentalists, they might not have needed my services.

Over the next few months, my involvement with Greenpeace UK died down somewhat. As my work was very task-specific, it depended on action and training. After the New Year, they were focusing more on research than direct action and any campaigns were being planned for later in the year. There wasn't enough for me not having to worry about alternatives. But this suited me fine. Although I would only be paid when the work merited it, I made sure I was a regular presence in the Islington office. I didn't want them to think I only showed my face when the controversial stuff happened. I wanted them to think I was one of them, eager to help out as and when required. It meant I'd always be on hand should the situation change and they needed help.

The lull in activity allowed me to concentrate on other clients. I knew that the undercover work – while fascinating – might not last forever. By that time, my involvement had lasted two years – much longer than I ever anticipated when I first encountered Alison for that driving course. It wasn't really sustainable on its own, however, and the situation with Greenpeace allowed me to look for other things.

I was still getting the odd job from the security consultants who'd set up the first Greenpeace job. At the same time, I undertook some test purchasing work on fake designer goods and perfumes. I went to Camden and bought a number of items, to take them to the client to examine. More often than not, they were fakes, or had been stolen, and the clients would take the necessary legal action to stop the rip-off items being sold. In these situations, companies are reluctant to go to the police and prefer to handle it in house with private prosecutions. There's an embarrassment factor attached to counterfeit goods, so the firms would rather bring in outside commercial contractors to do their work for them. If it gets into the press that a lot of designer goods are being ripped off it doesn't look good and they prefer to keep a lid on it.

Other work came from haulage companies that were having problems with drivers going off their routes and fitting in odd jobs when they should be working. My job was to carry out surveillance on the errant drivers and find out if they were doing anything dodgy. It's sad when companies spy on their own employees or contractors but often the suspicions of management were not without foundation. I supplied a dossier of evidence and it was up to them to act on it.

For some months, I was kept busy after a firm of solicitors contacted me, asking if I would be a professional witness to examine a personal injury claim that happened in Afghanistan. A driver had been left brain-damaged after an accident and his claim against the private company he worked for centred on the assertion that he hadn't received adequate training. I had to examine the circumstances and give my opinion whether that was the case and whether the appropriate safeguards had been in place. I was retained by the solicitors to produce a detailed report into the incident and the background. It was clear to me the company was negligent. I was registered as an expert witness on behalf of the claimant. Before it came to court, the defendants were served with my statement, some 30 pages long. Not long afterwards, a settlement was offered and the case was concluded without me having to give evidence in court.

It was some months after the Downing Street job when my next assignment with Greenpeace came. And it was to be another foreign adventure.

CHAPTER 12

PEACE CAMP

In my dealings with Special Branch, I often referred to them as UK PLC, though that is really the security services. Yet, SB might have been police but they were they were so political in their outlook they sometimes felt like an extension of the government.

These days, the term Special Branch has been replaced by Counter Terrorism Command but the name still carries a special significance in UK policing. After the first SB was formed in London in 1883 (to combat the Irish Republican Brotherhood incidentally), every force across the UK adopted its own unit to focus on intelligence gathering, mostly of a political or terrorist nature.

Concerning itself with matters of national importance, Special Branch grew into an international concept, with countries across the Commonwealth adopting specialised units to target major threats.

In the UK, as the intelligence relating to threats to national security were increasingly tackled by the security services – MI5 and MI6 – it was felt the unit was best utilised by merging with counterterrorism teams. In 2006, in the Metropolitan Police, SB merged with the Anti-Terrorist Branch, to form SO15 (Counter Terrorism Command), when the threat of terrorism from individual extremists and terror cells became the biggest risk facing national security on these shores.

Although Islamic fundamentalists and other extremists posed more of a threat than other traditional foes, as shown by the London bombings of 7 July 2005 when 52 innocent civilians were killed, there was still a keen interest in other groups. The protests that accompanied the G8 summit at Gleneagles in Scotland just as the bombs were going off, showed that global protest groups could cause widespread disruption.

Greenpeace might have had a rather hippy reputation but its capacity to embarrass governments and win popular support from the public was undimmed in 2006. And, with the release of Al Gore's provocative film, *An Inconvenient Truth*, that year, climate change and global warming were, if you excuse the term, hot topics. Intelligence was the key to protect against Islamic extremists or environmentalists and anything that could give the government an advantage in knowing how these organisations thought and what they were planning had to be considered a bonus.

Which is why I was left frustrated when my SB contacts seemed so reluctant to incentivise a trip I'd discovered could unearth a treasure trove of intelligence on the entire Greenpeace organisation. My links with Greenpeace International had remained strong. Although much of my time was spent forging relations with Greenpeace UK, I had made sure I kept up contact with Alison.

In March 2006, I was about to head out to Trinidad for six weeks to train the West Indian Special Branch (an example of how the British system of specialised policing was adopted in other Commonwealth countries) in anti-hijack driving skills, when Alison emailed me to sound me out about another trip overseas. She asked if I would be prepared to go to Turkey for an in-depth training course with dozens of other international members from Greenpeace offices worldwide, including many of the leading players.

The training camp was at the end of April. I was amazed to be invited but was initially unsure what role I'd be expected to play.

'You can add great value to our training regime,' she said. 'It's a nine-day training camp and you can brief our senior staff on the techniques you gave lessons on in Brazil. It's the perfect opportunity for you and it will benefit us greatly. I'll introduce you to Tim and Elizabeth, who head our research and intelligence.'

It was an incredible opportunity, which would take me to the heart of the international organisation. I would be able to probe even deeper into this world-famous activist group at a level far surpassing Greenpeace UK and it would place me firmly among the higher echelons of this organisation. This was a true infiltration assignment, one that should provide a very damning and previously unobtainable wave of intelligence that would be passed among all the European police offices, giving immense credit to British SB in the process. Naturally, I said yes in an instant and went straight to SB with my news.

Initially, I was offered a few hundred pounds to pull off this latest infiltration, but what was on offer had far bigger intelligence value than that; plus, I was due to go to Trinidad to train the West Indian Special Branch in anti-hijack driving for six weeks and stood to make just under £6000 from that trip, which was for my own business. SB had to do a lot better than that for a week's work in Turkey. Right up until the day I went to Turkey, it was stalemate over money, but I was given a quiet assurance that I would get what I had asked for and that SB was playing mind games, hoping to get me on the cheap. Nothing different there, I thought and that just typified the British government. They want everything for nothing, no matter whether it was your livelihood that was at risk.

'It sounds great,' said Terry. 'Go and glean all you can.'

I hated to bring up the subject of money. It would be great to take on these assignments safe in the knowledge that you were doing it for Queen and country. But even James Bond took a salary and information was a marketable commodity. SB offered me a modest sum and asked me to gather what I could for them.

'You don't seem happy with that,' Terry said, correctly reading my thoughts. I'd never made an issue about money before – and, after Downing Street, had been delighted with the bonus payments received for my hard work. I felt this was a unique opportunity, however.

'It's just that I feel this is a chance to collate information like never before. This would be intelligence you could distribute throughout Europe, the world even. Think of the kudos you'd be getting.'

'Times are tough,' Terry said. 'Every penny's got to be accounted for. There's an element of a fishing expedition here. We don't know yet how successful it could be. Why don't you go and see how you get on?'

It was typical from SB and the British government. They are content to play mind games with agents, knowing that the hapless operatives often have no choice but to take what they are given, even though they might be risking their lives or at least detection to get what's needed. On this occasion, I was made to sweat until the point I departed for Turkey over what I could expect to receive. It wasn't that long ago that they were praising me to the rafters for the intelligence I provided. Now, I felt there was an element of them taking me for granted.

Despite their reticence to place a value on the job, they were clearly interested in the potential of the trip. Terry and Martin at one stage even wanted to go to Turkey themselves because they were thinking that, if the intelligence was valuable enough, it would be passed on to Interpol, as I suggested. Turkey not being part of the EU caused problems, however. There was no agreement for foreign police officers to operate in the country. There was even a reluctance early on to even mention to the Turkish authorities what we were planning. Instead my point of contact in case things went horribly wrong was the Special Branch 'in country' officer, attached to the British Embassy.

As the day of departure approached, Alison contacted me again, to say I was travelling with another Brit, Allan Moss. I was slightly wary because Allan was from Greenpeace UK and, at that point, I'd been happy to keep my dealings with each of the organisations separate. There was nothing I could do on this occasion. I would just have to ensure that I kept my cards even closer to my chest than usual.

We met up in the departure lounge at Heathrow, while we waited for the flight to Istanbul. I made my last contact with SB while stocking up in Duty Free. I had never met Moss before but, as we got acquainted on the flight, I formed the opinion that he was a good guy and that we would get along without too much trouble. He was a fairly quiet character and was pleasant enough, but it was never my intention to make life-long friendships with people I encountered on undercover jobs. I was there to gain information. If you deviate from your mission and form friendships that aren't designed to supply you with information you're in trouble.

A taxi picked us up from the airport and drove us across town to the offices of Greenpeace Turkey, in the heart of town. Immediately, I assumed my surveillance mode and absorbed the layout of the office. It's amazing the type of detail that can come in handy to law enforcement agencies. I made a note of things like the strength of the door, building security and floor plans. I did this so it could be passed on to the Turkish authorities as a sweetener. At some stage, there was going to be an exchange of information.

Should Greenpeace's action plans increase in Turkey the country's police might want to raid the premises. If that happened, it would be invaluable for them to know what awaited them inside the building.

Very quickly, I saw that the Greenpeace mentality making everyone feel welcome and the fostering of a community spirit in evidence around the world. As in Brazil, I was greeted by Turkish members smiling broadly, while handing me a cold beer. They knew how to win me over!

I began the task of cultivating my potential sources of information and engaged some of the guys there about who was in charge and who we could expect to be attending the nine-day camp. I'd grown used to people asking me about my relationship with Alison, how I knew her and what roles I'd performed for Greenpeace, since I'd started working for them some four years earlier.

The following day, we would be departing for the campsite, some 100 km from Istanbul on the coast, so there was not much more I could do on the first night. It would be a three-hour drive to Woodyville, the camp where we'd be staying. I wasn't looking forward to the drive but I consoled myself with the knowledge that once we arrived there would be host of important people from whom I could glean information.

Woodyville was essentially a small ranch holiday camp, booked exclusively for Greenpeace International, but it was infinitely more comfortable than the Farm in Brazil. It comprised a series of wooden low-level houses with a diner-cum-bar. As you'd expect with Greenpeace, the setting was relaxing and chilled.

On our arrival, we had a quick meal and we were then allocated our wooden homes for the next five days. I was sharing with a Turkish bloke who seemed to be able to speak little English. I wasn't going to be complacent however. I knew of people who let slip secrets or compromised their position by saying too much in front of someone they believed couldn't speak a word of English.

In all, there were around 30-odd members of various ranks present, from all over the world, and it was clear that I could not commit my intelligence to paper through fear of being caught. Mostly, I would have to rely on my memory but I had another trick up my sleeve. Before I'd left the country, I'd arranged with SB to get up a 'secret strap'. A strap was a small logbook that would keep a record of messages I sent myself. As I didn't have either the time or the privacy to keep detailed notes, I could send myself text reminders to complete when I returned to the UK.

Although the accommodation should have been more comfortable than the tree huts in Brazil, I endured a disturbed night's sleep. I woke and made my way down to breakfast and began to mingle. The first meeting of the morning consisted of the allocation of training rooms and groups. The course had members from literally every country in Europe. The syndicates for training were broken into squads as follows. There was the research, intelligence and investigation squad, which was where I was to be; a boat training squad; a climbing squad; and a NVDA (non-violent direct action) training squad. Each would have specialised training in their chosen field for the five days to enhance their respective offices upon their return.

Having broken off into our groups, I went to the room where the researcher training was to happen and began gelling with the team of about 20, including Allan Moss. The first few hours were just an introduction as to what was going to take place but running this were the heads of research for the entire Greenpeace group – Tim, who was half Canadian, and Elizabeth, who was German.

From the off, the atmosphere was convivial but also organised and professional. Everyone knew their role and when they weren't attending a training session they had the laptops out, carrying our research and liaising with their home office. People were keen to meet and exchange stories and I was pleased to see dozens of photos being taken of nearly everyone at the camp. The official pictures I wanted to get hold of but the camaraderie and openness allowed me to snap away, taking pictures of my own without any questions asked.

Two activists who weren't so forthcoming – certainly from the photo point of view – were two from the Middle East. One, nicknamed Jesus because of his uncanny resemblance to Christ, was from Israel. The other, Hazim, was from Lebanon. They were close friends but, given the animosity between the countries, were very guarded and wary of word getting back to their respective homelands because of the problems their friendship would create. They could both expect to receive extreme punishment had they been seen to associate with each other. Despite this, they were united in their frustration at how pointless things were and the invisible sanctions that were placed on them. I got on well with them both but, when I asked to take their picture, they refused. I gently persisted and Jesus relented, but only if I agreed not to post the picture online or allow it to go public in any way.

Seeing the commitment of Jesus and Hazim, it struck me what a positive force Greenpeace could be on a global scale. It existed without borders and, when it channelled its energies in the right manner, was an effective agitator against national governments and corporations.

It's also what made it so good to spy on!

CHAPTER 13

THE HONEYTRAP

It was Tim who first raised the alarm. He called an emergency meeting in the canteen just before lunch. Everyone wore worried looks on their faces. No one could imagine what the drama was.

'I'm sorry to say,' he began, 'that we fear we have been infiltrated.'

My heart skipped a beat.

There was an audible gasp from some members.

Tim went on: 'We think we have someone spying on us in our midst.'

This is it, I thought. I've been rumbled. Maybe my whole invitation to this event was a ruse to expose me. I started to sweat.

'We think it's a foreign journalist. It could be a team, trying to dig up dirt on us.'

That sparked a buzz of excited chatter around the room. One wag shouted, 'We'll give them something to write about all right.'

The laughter helped break the tension.

My sphincter started to relax. Maybe this wasn't about me after all.

'We think they're posing as holidaymakers at the far end of the camp,' Tim said. 'We can't be sure but we know they are not part of our group. We just want to bring them to everyone's attention and, if you see anything or anyone suspicious, please let us know. Be careful also what you say and do around people you don't know.'

Phew! That was a close one.

No one seemed to know who the mystery hacks were, or if they indeed were journalists snooping on Greenpeace. As I felt I held the monopoly on any underhand covert surveillance in this camp, I was determined to root them out. If I was successful, it might put me in Tim's good books, which could make my time in here a lot easier.

The afternoon passed with more workshops and chatter about the unwelcome visitors died down. That night in the bar, I spied two men and a woman who I hadn't seen about the camp before. By the way they were dressed – in stylish casual clothes rather than backpacker gear – and their demeanour, I had a sneaky suspicion they might be the intruders Tim was talking about. They were trying a little too hard to be relaxed but were sitting on their own. I thought it an odd dynamic – two guys and a woman. She was pretty, with long dark hair and unless they enjoyed a *ménage à trois* of an evening, they made unconvincing holidaymakers, especially in a camp full of eco-warriors.

I sidled over and made my introductions. They claimed they were part of the climbing and boat squad. I doubted this straight away as I'd spent time with that group in the morning and hadn't seen these jokers.

I decided to play a little game and see where it led. I began to give the impression I was holding a lot of information about the set-up in the camp and how Greenpeace International was run. Instead, I fed them a lot of rubbish and wrong information. Their eyes lit up and they started buying me drinks like anyone's business. Within an hour, they were eating out my hand and lapping up any old nonsense I was giving them.

Not long after the men – called Marco and Alex – left the bar, leaving the brunette, who was getting prettier by the pint, with me. Her name was Monique and as much as I'd love to say she was interested in me for my rugged good looks and scintillating wit, I was convinced she was laying on a classic 'honeytrap', to glean more information from me. It's a very old trick but one that can be very effective, particularly in a setting like this when men are away from home, the drink is flowing and there are secrets to be had. Without giving the game away, I settled into character and played the role of an extremely flattered bloke eager to see where this encounter might lead.

Monique was a skilled operator, I'll give her that. Her English was good but she spoke with an accent that made her sound like Sophia Loren. She continued to ply me with drink and, the merrier I appeared to become, the more flirtatious she became. Subtly, her hands brushed mine, her big puppy-brown eyes gazed directly into mine and the flicks of her hair became more pronounced. She didn't lay on the interrogation thick but preferred to tease the information out of me. I continued to feed her guff information but at no time did she give any indication other than that she believed it to be real.

The whole situation amused me greatly. Here I was, working for SB against Greenpeace, and then working for Greenpeace against the international press – what a situation: it was win–win all the way for me; I couldn't lose!

Next, she moved in for the kill. Seductively draining her glass of wine, she rose from her seat and purred: 'I'm just going to freshen up.'

As I appeared to hang on her every word, she added, 'I'm going to head back to my room. Would you care to join me?'

Any normal man would have probably thought, fuck it, and abandoned any self-control for the promise of a bit of action. I, on the other hand, was only getting started on my mission. While Monique was in the Ladies', I grabbed Tim.

'I think I might have found your little problem,' I said. 'Leave it with me. I'm confident I'll get to the bottom of it within the hour.'

Clearly surprised, he sat there bemused. With a smile, he said, 'Thanks, Ross. I guess I'll leave you to it then.'

I returned to the table and, to my delight, saw that she'd left her clutch bag behind when she'd gone to the toilet. Not being in the United Kingdom and having no UK law to worry about, I rifled through her bag. It didn't take me long to find what I was looking for – an Italian press pass in her name, with a photo!

So, Tim was right. And I had rumbled them. I could have

confronted her there and then, when she returned from the toilet, but, by then, I was having too much fun to stop. Plus, I was curious to see how far she would push it!

Keeping hold of the press pass, I stuffed the rest of her belongings back into her bag and returned it to where I'd found it.

When she came back, I looked as keen as a dog on heat, got up, and said, 'Shall we?'

She smiled, picked up her bag, and winked suggestively as she tucked her T-shirt into her jeans. I got up, waved to a few lads who probably thought I'd won the World Cup and disappeared up the dirt track with her. As we got to her cabin, she asked me if I would like a bottle of wine. I agreed. She dimmed the lighting, produced a bottle of red and two glasses and came over to join me on the sofa.

For a moment, I thought she was seriously going to go through with this. She was a full-on seductress. As tempted as I was to see how far she would actually push it, I decided to go easy on her and gave her an opportunity to extricate herself from the situation – partly at least.

'Hey,' I said. 'Where did your friends go? Do you want to get them over too and we can have a bit of a party?'

It was hard to tell if she was genuinely frustrated or relieved by my suggestion. Within minutes – probably because they'd been on standby in a neighbouring cabin waiting for her signal, Marco and Alex arrived. We sat talking for a while. The conversation returned to the topics we'd been covering earlier in the evening but this time it really did feel I was under interrogation. They wanted to know my role in Greenpeace, how long I'd been with them, whether this type of camp took place every year, who the main players were, what NVDAs were on the agenda. Once again, I span them a tangled weave of fibs.

I was tempted to finish the wine with them but I felt it was time to call a halt to this game of charades. I excused myself and went to use the toilet. Getting the press pass out of my pocket, I tucked it up my sleeve and returned to the others. When I returned, Monique smiled and looked set to refill my glass and continue with the Spanish, or should that be Italian Inquisition.

'Do you have a light for a cigarette please?'

'Sure,' she said, reaching for her bag. She opened it and I could see the lighter. I grabbed it but also made it appear I'd seen and snatched the press pass. Holding it up like some prized trophy, I turned to Marco and Alex and said, 'I take it you won't be joining us for breakfast then?'

Their faces dropped with sheer horror and embarrassment. They had no response and the fact that they didn't even try to offer an excuse or explanation told me all I needed to know. I thought about hanging around to see if they came up with a plausible cover story, but they looked so dumbstruck that I casually picked up the bottle of wine and walked out, laughing.

It was such a buzz, burning these journos at their own game. I called Tim on his mobile. He was chilling out down by the beach. I met him down there. He started laughing when he saw me with the bottle of wine.

'So, what did you find out?' he said.

'Italian journos,' I said. 'Three of them. You were right. They were posing as Greenpeace activists, though, not holidaymakers. They spent the whole night pumping me for information. Don't worry, though, I didn't give away any state secrets.'

Tim looked stunned. It was almost as if this was too much for him to take in at once.

I went on: 'I found their press passes. I don't think they'll be troubling you any more this week though. You should have seen the looks on their faces. Priceless.'

Tim couldn't stop laughing. 'Wow,' he said, scarcely believing what I was telling him. 'It sounds like we owe you one.'

'Shame,' I added. 'I was beginning to think I was on to a good thing there, too.'

We sat on the beach and polished off the rest of the wine. It was safe to say I was now Tim's golden boy. My credibility was through the roof. On covert jobs, you dream of scenarios like that when you can ingratiate yourself to the people you're trying to infiltrate in a completely natural way. He didn't suspect a thing now where I was concerned. And, given I was in Turkey to lecture Greenpeace staff on deception, effectively, and covert techniques, I'd just proved I was an expert in the field at detecting impostors.

It was a good job they didn't have someone as experienced as me on their books, I thought.

The following day, my antics were the talk of the whole camp and the journalists were the butt of much laughter and jokes. Breakfast was especially satisfying. Even more so when Tim came over while I was eating.

'You probably won't be surprised to hear this,' he said, 'but the journalists have checked out already. They'd cleared out by 5 a.m. They paid their bill – including your astronomical bar bill – and scarpered. Nice work, my friend.'

With an endorsement like that, the people at my table were looking on in awe. This was a major result.

'I'm looking forward to your lecture even more now,' Tim said. 'It's good to have you here.'

I then settled down for the day's lectures with a glowing feeling deep inside, my job now, I hoped, made 100-per-cent easier by an hour of fun. Not taking this too far, I resorted back to my original task of getting intelligence for SB, and not Greenpeace.

People might question how I can switch loyalties like that but they have to remember that all the way along I've always provided a service to whomever I'm working for. Over the years, Greenpeace received the benefit of my experience and know-how, built up over years of training with the army and the police. In return, the authorities that developed those skills are kept informed of what this group are up to. It's a fair trade off, in my opinion.

Situations like that honeytrap sting are what you live for. They keep you on your toes. Some people have asked me if I have ever suffered an identity crises. I always say, 'Only at weekends, when my name's Veronica!'

All's fair in love and war and, when you're in the field, you use any means at your disposal to keep one step ahead. Only two days in and Turkey was shaping up to be a worthwhile exercise. I momentarily cursed SB for being slow to appreciate the value of coming here but quickly shrugged it off. I was used to disproving their scepticism by now. Besides, I had a lot of work to do.

That day in Woodyville was full on – nearly 12 hours of meetings, seminars, discussions and training. I was privy to so much useful intelligence it was a struggle to remember it all – even for the text message updates I was sending myself via SB.

The keeping of detailed notes during the discussions was frowned upon by the Greenpeace International chiefs but I collared Tim and asked if he minded if I kept very sketchy notes. I figured he'd cut me some slack after my success unmasking the journos and by asking his permission it meant if anyone found my scribblings I'd be above suspicion.

'That's fine,' he said. 'Just make sure it's nothing that could be intelligible if it falls into the wrong hands, particularly if you're searched at the airport.'

That was fine by me but his attitude showed how concerned Greenpeace was as an organisation. I smiled inwardly, reminded of the old adage: 'Just because you're paranoid doesn't mean they're not out to get you.'

That night, I was glad of the notes. We finished the business at around 9 p.m. and went upstairs, where a few cases of beer were being downed by the all the groups that had come together for a session to let off some steam. Music was blaring and people were already bopping on the dance floor.

Although I never consider myself to be off-duty, I was settling into the beer after a long day and was mentally retiring for the night when Elizabeth collared me. She started by wanting me to tell her about the events of the previous night, which I duly did.

Then, however, she changed gear and started asking me about Tilbury Docks in Essex. It was the principal port for London. All the big container ships docked there carrying everything from food to vehicles. She said they were targeting containers there and asked if I could help Greenpeace International with a bit of surveillance. I could have told her there and then that it would be a difficult watch, with tight security. The port might not be an obvious terrorist target but precautions were certainly in place and they'd be on the lookout for anyone disrupting business in a busy port.

I told her I'd be happy to help and her request further confirmed to me how well I was in there with them.

The following day was extremely valuable. I sat in on more lectures for the research and intelligence group. I was impressed by the sophistication of their expertise. Advice was given on cover stories to get into buildings, how to monitor shipping and emergency beacons, IT interrogations, and collecting websites and passwords to sources outside of Greenpeace, sources that were known as 'friendly'.

The IT expert was Pete, who would be the first to admit he was a class-A geek, but a fascinating chap. He was a computer whiz. I hooked up with him and he gave me IT programs that would encrypt, decrypt, and decode information, and he explained how to use them. Pete was so security conscious it was unreal.

He wore very thick glass lenses so he would not be identified by airport biometric systems. He also revealed that Greenpeace had a fair amount of insider intelligence within the police and coastguard that provided information to the organisation.

My lecture fed directly into this realm. To the group that contained Tim and Elizabeth, I gave advice on countersurveillance, tradecraft, CROPs (covert rural observation points) and tricks on how to circumvent security systems. I'd like to think the lessons were mutually beneficial.

Two days before the conclusion of the course, I was invited to a private party, where a lot of the senior figures got together for a drink away from the ground-level guys. This was interesting in itself because, so far, in my experience of Greenpeace, they did their best to eschew any hierarchical system, when clearly it existed in the same way as many organisations.

Chatting to some of their Middle Eastern operatives, I was shown passports that had double pages and were heavily tampered with to mask over several visits they had made, mainly between offices in neighbouring countries. A lot of these places were no-go areas and too much travel would have been an excuse for border guards to block entry, particularly between Israel and Palestine. To get round this, passports were doctored. Some activists had two passports – one 'clean' and one used for travelling to areas where there would not be a problem.

Greenpeace UK might have objected to the snooping on its activities that I was doing but it was nothing compared to the tight controls that would be imposed on activists if other countries knew what they were up to.

The party was raging into the wee small hours and I faced a dilemma. I was keen to stay up and see it through because the later it gets the more people can be inclined to talk and that's when they can let slip more radical thoughts and disclose potential targets I wouldn't otherwise hear about. However, having been on the go for nearly 20 hours, I was flagging and I was worried that I might inadvertently let something slip, or recklessly text an update to the SB strap when someone was looking.

People were chatty – although whether it was

meaningful was open to debate – and the fact that there were still a lot of people hanging about convinced me to stick it out a bit longer.

Believe it or not, it's hard to abstain, especially at a Greenpeace party. I pretended I'd nodded off, to avoid having to come up with another excuse. Eventually, though, someone shook me and urged me to get to bed so I took it as a sign to call it a day. By the time I got to my room, it was 4.45 a.m. and my head felt light but my limbs heavy.

I was nearing the end of my time in Turkey. While pleased with my success, I was relishing the chance it was giving me to test my skills. It would prove to be good practice for what was to come.

CHAPTER 14

A RACE AGAINST THE CLOCK

I knew what I wanted to get my hands on. I just had to work out a way to get it.

Tim had whetted my appetite in the morning – of what was our last day – by revealing the existence of hundreds of photos taken over the week. I'd seen people snapping away during my time at the camp and I knew many of those would be used for official Greenpeace International purposes, but I didn't appreciate how many images there were. Hundreds, Tim had said, showing everyone who had attended camp, the leaders of the international movement, plus their intelligence and research heads, action chiefs, boat captains, the lot. It was a veritable treasure trove.

'Many of you can access the pictures,' Tim had told us as we congregated for the final exercise of the week – a mock scenario where we were able to demonstrate the skills we'd learned. 'They will be available at some point in the future on a secure website, where you can apply for a series of passwords.'

Secure website? Series of passwords? That wasn't going to suit me at all. I couldn't afford to wait. I needed those photos now. I only had a few hours left of our final day to do it. I had to go back with them, no matter what I had to do to get my hands on them. I hadn't yet made SB aware of their existence. If I didn't get them, there would be no fall-out, but I had placed a lot of stock in this trip and, if I could round it off with a complete pictorial dossier of the hierarchy within Greenpeace International, I was sure it would go down well with my handlers. The pressure I felt was only that which I put on myself. After the success of the Downing Street operation, this would really strengthen my position for future operations, I hoped.

There was little point in thinking too far ahead though. First, I had to work out a plan and that involved working out who exactly had the images and where. Throughout the day, I busied myself on the final task and joined in with the rest of the activists as planned. It felt as though my last night in Turkey could be my biggest challenge yet on my adventure with Greenpeace – even more than the hostage situation in Brazil, or the dumping of coal at Number 10. I really felt that, if I could pull this stunt off, I would truly have made the transition from upholder of the law to undercover agent.

As the day wore on, I still hadn't come up with a plan. I had to think of something soon or I'd simply run out time. If I didn't manage to do this tonight I could forget about it. I wouldn't be getting them at a later date.

Over dinner in the canteen, I contemplated my sourcing of the photos. From making discreet inquiries, I found the names of two people who had the entire album. Crucially, they had received all the photos before anything had been said about the restrictions placed on them. After I'd finished eating, I went to find them. One, Mark, from the Netherlands, was drinking in the bar. The other, an IT geek called Joe, was working on his computer in the lecture room, which was just adjacent to the bar.

A germ of an idea was forming in my mind. For it to work, however, I needed to get my hands on a laptop. I thought of Allan Moss, my fellow Brit. His eye had been off the ball since about the second day, when he fell for the charms of a young Israeli worker. I caught him on his way to the bar to meet her.

'Hey, Allan, can I use your laptop for half an hour, to check my emails, please?' I asked.

'Sure, yes, come, I'll get it for you.'

'Cheers, mate,' I said. 'You're a big help.'

He retrieved his laptop and I took it to the lecture room, where Joe and a number of other activists were busy working away. I was still a long way off from my plan working and I wasn't even sure if I could get my hands on what I needed. However, the lecture room was where the IT guru, Pete, hung out most of the time and I figured if anyone had what I required it would be him. He wasn't around but, by his desk, I spied what I was looking for – laptop link leads.

I casually strolled around the room to Pete's desk and picked up the leads and returned to my seat. I sat there in front of Moss's laptop, waiting for my opportunity. It was tense, it was touch-and-go, and it was damn risky. I would only get one chance at this.

My target was Joe's computer. It was his laptop that held the photos and these were the images I could put names to, not only for the UK police but for Interpol and similar police agencies throughout the Western world, and possibly the Middle East, as well. No one had been able to identify the main players together in one place and at one time with up-to-date images. This had been the ultimate gathering of the top minds and brains of the entire organisation, and the images of everyone here were only minutes away from my clutches.

The situation was simple. I had a laptop in a room with laptop link leads and, twelve feet away, was my target computer. The only trouble was, Joe was using his laptop and wasn't showing any signs of taking a comfort break. There were seven others in the room, quietly beavering away. Moss was otherwise engaged but, at some point, he would come back for his computer, so I didn't have all night. Some operations work best when you wait for the right opportunity and strike when it presents itself but, other times, you have to make things happen. I had the feeling this was one of those times.

So, how the hell do I do this? I had an advantage in that, over the past week, I'd built up such a level of trust that no one would suspect me of foul play. The events over the past few days had shown I was one of them. In fact, if anything, I was more hardcore, willing to raid a handbag to expose a snooping journalist. That knowledge reassured me and I felt strangely calm. I had clarity of thought. Now, I needed to formulate the next stage of the plan and the intelligence would be mine.

Then it came to me. It would require balls and some degree of luck. I had the former. I had to trust I'd get a degree of the latter. I decided to totally front the situation. Any flapping around by me would cause attention and, knowing my relationship with these people, they were likely to come over and help. I had to be confident, bold, and push my luck entirely.

I stood up walked over with Moss's laptop in one hand, with the case containing the laptop links in the other and sat straight down, bold as anything, at the desk next to Joe.

He looked up and smiled. 'You OK?'

'Yes,' I said, 'only I'm having problems opening a program. Do you think you could help me?'

I said the program I was trying to use was Torpark, a proxy server that hides your real Internet service provider or ISP. It was something Pete had given us that week. Ever helpful, Joe took the laptop and started working on the program. This was now my reason for moving next to him.

Naturally, it took him a matter of moments to open the program. Ever grateful, I offered to buy him a drink by way of thanks.

'Erm, yeah,' he said. 'OK. I just need to go to the toilet, though. Do you mind watching my computer?'

'Be happy to,' I said. I couldn't believe my luck. What do they say? Fortune favours the brave?

'Tell you what,' I said, 'why don't you go to the bar while you're up. Here's the cash.' I handed him some money. 'Mine's a pint,' I added, somewhat cheekily, given what I was about to do.

Once he had cleared the door, I plugged in the lap-link cables without even stopping to think and then set about finding the files containing the images on his computer. I glanced around just to check no one was eyeballing me. They were all engrossed on their own screens.

I scanned Joe's desktop and found the file I was looking for. There were over 450 images. Holy fuck! I just had to pray it wouldn't take an age to copy. It took a second to click on the right options and start the transfer. All the images should now be copying to Moss's laptop.

I scanned the room again, an excuse at the ready should anyone ask if I needed help, but, again, no one even so much as looked up. There was still a chance someone could see the cables and wonder what the hell I was doing. In these situations sometimes it's better to be upfront. Rather than skulk about, create a distraction – that way people are less likely to pay attention to the small details, funnily enough.

'Hey, anyone want a drink?' I said to no one in particular but to the room in general. A few of them looked up. 'Come on, it is our last night.'

I got a few mumbled requests and smiles. It was enough. I got my mobile out and rang Joe. He was still at the bar. I passed on the order, telling him I'd pop through to give him a hand in a moment. He seemed none the wiser. Why would he be? It was just good old Ross being friendly on the last night.

While I was on the phone to him, relaying the drinks, I looked at his screen. I needed about two more minutes for the file to copy. Christ, how long did it take to copy a few pictures. I started to curse Greenpeace for taking so many.

Come on, come on, hurry up. The percentage bar didn't seem to be moving. The transfer meter was reading 70 per cent, but it had been stuck on that for an eternity. I kept looking towards the door. Joe was going to be back any second. Hurry the fuck up, I wanted to scream at the computer. The calmness I'd been feeling earlier was evaporating steadily. My insides were boiling, my palms sweaty. I tried to look relaxed, leaning back in my chair absent-mindedly swinging back and forth as if I didn't have a care in the world and was just contentedly waiting for my drink to arrive. Everyone's eyes were back on their screens. The ceiling fan above me whirred. Come on you fucking useless computer.

The percentage edged to 75 per cent. I wasn't going to make it. I looked back at the door. Fuck, Joe was approaching with the drinks. As he came in the doorway, I instinctively pointed over his shoulder. I didn't even know what I was doing – just anything to stop him coming over to the computers. He stopped and looked around.

'Someone was calling, Joe,' I said. 'You've not come away without my change, have you?' They hadn't, but what the hell, I was nearly there.

Joe paused for a second, then turned and made to go back towards the bar. The transfer bar read 95 per cent. Two more seconds. Joe clearly thought better of it, perhaps remembered that of course he'd picked up the change. He turned around. Transfer complete.

'Careful there, Joe,' I said, getting up and blocking his view of the desks. Behind my back, I unhooked the leads and stuffed them in my back pocket. I'd done it, without a second to spare.

'Thanks, Joe,' I said, finally feeling I could exhale. 'You're a good mate.'

I made to leave but then had one last brainwave. It was

insanely cheeky, but also necessary on my part. I had the images but I had to copy them again so I could get them off Moss's laptop and onto something I could hand to SB.

'One more favour, please, Joe?' I asked. 'You don't have a spare CD I could have please? It would be great to copy the program in case I lose it.'

Not only had I just nicked the photos from his computer but now I was asking him for a CD to load them onto. Joe duly obliged and handed me a disc. Job done. Within seconds, the images were copied, the CD safely locked away, the laptop back with Moss and I was in the bar having a well-earned pint within half an hour of setting my plan in motion. And the best part? No one was any the wiser.

That night, I got well and truly pissed. I considered it a night off after all my hard work. I sent my final strap text to SB, reporting some good news. I'd fill them in on the details on my return to England.

Several hours later, at Heathrow, I parted company with Moss and breathed a heavy sigh of relief as I confidently strolled through immigration and customs with my bag of goodies.

I could finally relax and start the normalisation process that most undercover agents go through in one form or another. This process is a period of time post-operation, where your mind and body adjust to a normal practice and routine, hopefully providing resettlement of the mind. The impact from this job left me tired, drained, and with a scrambled head with all the information I had collated. It is essential for most operatives to relax if they want to stay on top of the facts. If you don't, you can easily find yourself forgetting a lot of what you were supposed to remember. I decided to give myself two days rest before I even started thinking about my report to SB.

Luckily, I had the text strap notes I'd sent myself during the week. These proved invaluable in jogging my memory and making sure I didn't miss out any of the important stuff. When I added my own personal photos to the ones I'd retrieved from Joe's computer, I discovered I had over 480 images. Each of these I had to describe and caption, identifying all of the main players on each of them. Then I had to compile a detailed debrief report about the camp, the set-up of the organisation and how it was run.

It took me four days to compile my report and go through the images. Within the week, a meeting was set up in a Dartford hotel with Terry and Martin, my SB handlers, to go through every piece of information I had included in the file. I'd even indexed the photos to correspond with the pages in the report. A bloody thorough job, I thought. Thankfully, so too did SB. They couldn't believe I'd provided so much information. It took us six hours to go through all the report and the photographs.

'Fucking hell,' said Terry. 'Nice work here, Ross. You're bloody born for this role, you know that.'

'This is unbelievable, Slater,' said Martin. 'We've never had this much information on any group, let alone Greenpeace.'

They vowed to pass it up the food chain. The information was in such a detailed state it could be passed to Interpol. They were delighted.

Also happy was Alison. A few weeks after I returned, she got in touch to ask how I'd found it.

'Very rewarding,' I said, without word of a lie.

'I hear you made quite an impact,' she said. 'I'm delighted

you could make it along. We're fortunate to have your expertise at our disposal.'

If only you knew, Alison, if only you knew.

Three years into my assignment with Greenpeace, I felt more at home with the double-agent role than ever. I felt like I couldn't fail. SB were happy with the intelligence. Greenpeace were happy with the expertise. What could possibly go wrong?

After a couple of weeks, feeling energised and rejuvenated, I rang Steve at Greenpeace UK.

'How's it going, buddy,' I said. 'Got anything for me?'

CHAPTER 15

OPERATION ENGLAND STARS

There were worse places to hang out, I supposed, but when I finally entered the Greenpeace UK action unit I imagined I'd be sent to more interesting locations than the leafy Surrey countryside.

When you think of the battlegrounds of the eco-warrior, you think nuclear power stations, the icy wastelands of the Arctic Circle and the Amazonian rainforest – not Chelsea Football Club.

Yet, here I was, sitting outside the training ground of the Premier League champions, in Cobham, waiting to spy on some of the best known faces in English football. Their crime? They drove Range Rovers and 4x4s, 'gas-guzzlers', as the tabloids liked to call them – or 'Chelsea tractors', ironically, given the vehicle's popularity in the well-heeled district of West London.

It was Gemma's idea. Some weeks earlier, she had called me in to the Boiler House to go through the details of her latest brainwave. She explained Greenpeace wanted to target those England footballers that irresponsibly drove these less environmentally friendly motors. I'd rarely seen her so enthusiastic. She had compiled a dossier of the worst offenders, but wanted me to add to the database by gathering as much information about some of the key players – what cars they drove, the registration numbers, their addresses, what their daily movements were like. She even wanted me to include their wives and girlfriends, the infamous WAGs, whose presence at the recent World Cup in Germany had caused so much consternation back home.

'If you can look after the Chelsea end,' she said, 'we'll have other units covering teams in Manchester and Liverpool.'

In these situations, I liked to adopt a respectful attitude, one that seemed receptive to her suggestion, while at the same time perhaps gently questioning the viability of the idea, without pissing on her chips completely.

'OK, and what do you propose we do once we've compiled all this information?' I said.

'Launch a coordinated protest,' she said. 'It will be a massive publicity stunt. We'll really get people thinking about what these cars do to the environment. Besides, no one has any sympathy for these players and their huge egos and vastly inflated salaries. It's a soft target but effective.'

She was certainly pleased with herself.

'OK, these are players who are used to being hounded by the press. What if they try to take evasive action and crash into an oncoming car?' I asked, playing devil's advocate.

She looked at me like I'd just burst her last balloon.

'I'm sure that won't happen. Let's just compile the info and take it from there.'

And so that was what found me outside Chelsea's state-of-the-art training facility in Cobham. It wasn't the easiest place to watch, with one dedicated entranceway to the complex. Sitting outside in a solitary car, you'd get spotted in seconds and it could look suspicious. However, I found a side road a little further back from the complex in which to sit and watch for the cars I wanted. Thankfully, the players didn't really alternate the cars they were driving too much, especially the lovers of their 4x4 Range Rovers, like Terry. What made the job easier was that Greenpeace had the home addresses of the key targets so if you lost one of them you could always revert to their home and try and pick them up there.

Each day, I chose a different target and if several of the players came out at the same time I'd choose the one I knew least about and follow him.

So far, I'd compiled dossiers on the team captain, John Terry, and his England team-mates, Frank Lamped and Ashley Cole. Another former Chelsea star, Dennis Wise, was also on my list. Gemma had provided me with addresses for a couple of them and the rest I'd found myself. Over the preceding weeks, I'd followed them to and from training, sat outside the club's stadium Stamford Bridge in Fulham on match days and, also, had compiled a fairly comprehensive dossier on their movements. I'd made cursory checks on the WAGs, noting what cars they drove, but some of them had small children and I wasn't comfortable following around women on their own.

It was somewhat ironic as, since the age of 11, I had

supported Chelsea and, before I joined the army, used to attend all the home games. I still kept up with their results but only really looked out for the big games. I knew all the players, however, so identification wasn't an issue. During the operation, I never went inside the ground, just kept observations from the outside or nearby, where I could best get a view of the players' entranceway. I knew from press reports and research who my targets were, but used to double-check before going out that day, to make sure no one had suddenly sprouted a beard or changed their hair colour. With footballers today, you could never be too careful.

Up north, other Greenpeace activists were doing the same with players like Wayne Rooney and Steven Gerrard. Certainly, carbon emissions were high on Greenpeace's agenda and so I could understand why these cars – and the famous people who drove them – became a target.

I was pleased to be given work that required me to be out on my own. It showed I was trusted. Yet, I couldn't help feeling this was one colossal waste of time. And, from a legal point of view, I felt I had an obligation and a duty of care to protect public life, so I notified SB of Greenpeace's interest. When I relayed the information, Terry shook his head, more out of resignation than anything else.

'How do you want to play it?' I asked.

'We'll need to let them know,' he sighed, clearly unimpressed that the revelation meant he had to do some work.

'You think?' I said. 'I'm sure I'll be told if it progresses to action stage. Maybe we could hold off until that point. No need to alarm anyone needlessly.'

'Nah,' he said. 'I think if high-profile players like these are under surveillance, we're duty bound to inform them. If anything should happen to them, or another member of the public, and it later emerges that we'd been informed but did nothing there would be hell to pay. It's not worth it.'

'Cover your arses, in other words,' I said.

'Precisely.'

In a week or so, I felt I'd done all I could as far as the surveillance was concerned. I knew where the WAGs did their shopping, had their hair done and liked to go for lunch. If any of them had been having an affair I would have known about it.

I compiled a report but painted a fairly bleak picture of the consequences should they try any kind of stunt. If they attempted it too close to the training ground or the stadium, they ran the risk of being spotted by the owner Roman Abramovich's personal bodyguards. These hulks were ex-SAS and if they became suspicious of any protest Greenpeace might have a skirmish on their hands. If you left it too close to the players' houses you'd lose them behind their gated communities. It was a nice idea but ultimately pointless.

I later discovered SB had tipped the players off. They told them they had someone on the inside so there was no need to worry. The advice they gave was to carry on as normal and they would be notified if the threat of action escalated. Given how miserably the team had performed at the World Cup in Germany, the last thing these guys needed was to be victims of a publicity stunt. I often wondered whether the protest would have gone ahead if Greenpeace had put anyone else on the surveillance, and if the England stars know how close they came to being ambushed by a bunch of eco-warriors.

If the Special Branch officers had a headache over the footballer campaign, it was nothing compared to their reaction when I informed them of Greenpeace's latest brainwave … because it was one that could have sparked an international incident.

It all began when Steve announced he wanted to deviate from the organisation's main focus for a short-term, quick-hit protest, which he hoped would make a political point. He knew that the US, with the exception perhaps of Nigeria, owed the most in unpaid congestion charge fees accrued by the country's ambassador and his diplomatic cars.

The congestion charge, a deeply unpopular tax, was imposed on Londoners in 2003. In an attempt to dissuade motorists from bringing their vehicles into the city centre, a charge of £5 applied in a certain designated area during certain times. As well as trying to reduce traffic congestion, one of the aims of the scheme was to improve air quality, something Greenpeace supported. The charge rose steadily over the next few years. Greenpeace discovered that the US embassy refused to pay the charge, claiming America did not pay taxes in foreign countries.

'We could have some fun and games with this,' Steve said when he told me the background. 'Let's block the ambassador's car.'

Immediately, he said it alarm bells started ringing.

Steve tasked me specifically with the surveillance because he knew I had expert knowledge of the target and the location, in Grosvenor Square, in Mayfair, where the embassy was situated. In 2001, I'd trained the whole fleet of embassy drivers, including the chauffeur to the ambassador himself, on tactical driving. I didn't need to go down there to scope the place out. I knew already this was a near-impossible spec. The cars were parked in an underground lot, where the passengers could get in and out without being seen. The vehicles emerged through two side ramps to the left and right of the main entrance. There was no chance of being able to block the cars when they weren't being used. The only hope would be to follow it to a location and try to block it there. Given the security around the ambassador, that would be suicidal.

When I told him the difficulties involved with trying to find the motors unattended, he looked at me as if I was mad.

'Nah, nah,' he said, 'we don't need to do that. We just need to know when it's likely to leave, which direction it's headed and we'll box it in from both sides. While he's sitting there wondering what's hit him, bang, we've got some great photos.'

Now it was my turn to look at him as though he was mad.

'Bang's the appropriate word,' I said. 'The ambassador is guarded by the FBI. They're armed at all times.'

'Don't be silly,' Steve said. 'They're not going to open fire on a bunch of protestors. It'll be easy. I'll run it on the ground on my motorbike. I'll just look like a million other despatch riders. We'll have a couple of teams on standby to react when we know what direction they're going then go for it.'

He was adamant. I guess, given his track record of daring missions and headline-grabbing stunts, he was better placed than anyone to gauge what you could and couldn't get away with. He'd been jailed in Washington for his trouble. I began to wonder if a few hours in the slammer might be considered a good result should this job go pear-shaped. In a box six feet under might be a more likely outcome.

His view was that, as I'd trained them, I would know how the drivers were likely to react. I tried to protest further but he cut me off.

'Look, just go down there, check on their movements and come back to me,' he said. 'How long do you need?'

I knew I needed to buy some time. I had a bad feeling about this plan. I asked for two weeks to give me some breathing space.

That night, I went straight on to Terry.

'We need to meet,' I said. 'We have a live situation that's potentially troublesome.'

The backsides nearly fell out of Terry and Martin's pants when I told them. Their jaws hit the floor.

'You are fucking kidding me,' Martin said.

'Have they lost their bloody minds?' Terry added.

I explained the whole set-up as Steve saw it – him acting as the mobile control unit, the other units to be standing off, covering other routes off such as Grosvenor Square to Park Lane, and the top end going to towards Oxford Circus. They sat there shaking their heads.

'Fuck, fuck, fuck,' said Terry. 'This is going to be a fucking bloodbath. You know how trigger-happy these Yanks are. They won't think twice about opening fire on someone blocking the ambo's car.'

'They're not exactly going to stop and ask which protest

group they belong to, are they?' said Martin. 'They'll just assume it's a bloody suicide bomber and take them out.'

'It'd be a bloody great international incident,' he added. 'There are no two ways about it.'

'Any idea how we handle it?' I said.

Martin and Terry exchanged looks before the Detective Sergeant spoke: 'It involves a foreign power so we have no choice but to run it through SB. The powers-that-be might want to bring in Six. I'd imagine they'll want to keep the government out of this though. No point risking this turning nuclear unless it needs to be.'

Wow, could they really be talking about bringing in MI6 and then, potentially, alerting the government? My instincts had told me it was serious situation and I was relieved they shared my concern but maybe this was bigger than even I imagined.

'If worst comes to the worst, we might have to make some pre-emptive arrests. Consider it a conspiracy. That would expose you, though, my friend. Not ideal,' said Martin.

They vowed to come back to me quickly. By now, I'd grown accustomed to SB time. It was why I'd asked Steve for two weeks to prepare. I was stunned when Terry came back to me within a day, requesting another meeting. The by now standard countersurveillance techniques observed, we sat down in another hotel near Tower Bridge.

Martin was straight to the point.

'Right, we've had conversations with the anti-terror unit and MI6. Everyone's in agreement. If this stunt goes ahead, there will be more guns on the ground than at the O.K. Corral.

'Someone's going to get hurt. We can't have US guards opening fire on the streets of London.'

'OK', I said. 'How do we do that?'

Terry and Martin exchanged one of their now trademark looks.

'You have to get it stopped,' Terry said.

'Me?'

'Yes, do what ever you have to,' Martin said, 'but just get it stopped. Tell them you've scoped the place out and they're tooled to the max. It will be carnage. Impress upon these cabbage-munchers that they won't see another sunrise if they push ahead with this. Isn't there a seal cub that needs saving somewhere?'

I got the message. I gave a rue smile at their brand of humour but it masked a deeper concern. Yes, they'd tolerate the antics of these well-meaning protesters but they could come down on them.

'Just do your best,' Terry said, as they made to leave. 'Let us know what their reaction it.'

Great, I thought, when I was outside and had a chance to digest what the situation was. They claim it's a possible international incident yet they want me to defuse it. It was a very precarious situation. I was surprised the Americans hadn't been told. Surely, it would have been better to put them on alert. I suppose SB couldn't trust the Americans to keep a lid on it. They might react to a car backfiring next to them or something. I'd do my best to dissuade Steve but what if he chose to ignore my advice and went ahead without me? I went home feeling very uneasy.

I made a point of seeing Steve the following day.

'Listen, I've had a chance to check this place out and it's

even more heavily guarded than I remembered. Must be a post-9/11 thing or something. Every driver and bodyguard is armed.'

Steve looked at me sceptically. 'So?' he said.

'So, they're not going to think twice about shooting if they think there's an attack on the ambassador.'

'We won't be looking like any suicide bomber or some anti-American nut. We'll make it clear who we are and what the protest is about. We can stick a banner over the car saying IMPOUNDED UNTIL YOU PAY YOUR CONGESTION CHARGE or something a bit more catchy.'

He wasn't grasping the seriousness of this situation at all.

'Look, you'll be dealing with the FBI, effectively. These guys are trained to react to terror situations. Boxing a diplomatic car in on a busy city street will be seen as a clear sign of aggression,' I said. 'They are trained to react with force.'

Steve still looked unconvinced.

'We're talking about an ambassador and they aren't going to give a shit about you. Look at it from their point of view. You don't believe who comes in your front door, so why should they believe you? You're not going to be able to run all over the ambassador's car.

'They are not going to wait to read your banner or take your details. They'll use reasonable force. And don't think you're going to have the UK government denouncing them for it either. We've stood shoulder to shoulder with Bush over terrorism. A year ago, we had our own terror attacks in London. Everyone is still jittery. In this climate, there's going to be little sympathy for environmentalists trying to score cheap political points,' I said.

Steve was silent for a bit. Perhaps he was stunned by the passion in my appeal.

'OK,' he said finally. 'You might be right. Does seem a bit risky.'

I looked at him quizzically. Was he really conceding so readily?

'You sure?' I said.

'Look, it was just going to be a bit of fun. I thought it might generate a cheap bit of publicity. It's not worth starting a war over. The Yanks have no sense of humour about these things – and I should know.

'Thanks for the heads-up.'

That was it. The plan, as quickly as it was devised, was scrapped. I was mightily relieved. I left Steve and called Terry to pass on the good news. But, heading home, I couldn't help wondering that maybe he was just bluffing me and still intended to go ahead to make his point. If that happened I'd be powerless to do anything to stop it.

However, I was sure SB had a contingency plan – a Plan B – if I hadn't managed to convince Steve. Surely, they wouldn't have let it happen.

CHAPTER 16

COPS AT WAR

Following my now fairly frequent operational meetings with SB, we would often retire to the nearest pub for a night of old bill banter, bad jokes and barrels of beer. Sometimes these nights would end in a massive bar bill and throbbing heads in the morning.

One day, Terry asked to meet me for a general intelligence update on both Greenpeace and some other projects that were running parallel to the environmentalist job. We met at Liverpool Street station in the city but, when our business concluded at 1.30 p.m., Terry suggested nipping to a boozer for lunch with one of his colleagues, Dave.

The bar was full of pretty-boy suits and office workers taking liquid lunches and generally misbehaving. We took ourselves into a corner and, while we had a couple of drinks, it wasn't a heavy session by our standards at least. We took our time ordering lunch and, as the bar thinned out after the lunchtime rush, we set the world to rights, discussing how much the police had changed in such a short period of time and had a general moan about factors outwith our control. We finished lunch but hung around for a couple more hours until such time as the bar started to fill up again with workers clocking off for the day.

The bar was staffed by British and foreign workers but I happened to notice a Russian bloke standing on the door. I thought he looked out of place given the clientele and the other staff but I also happened to notice that he wasn't wearing an SIA licence that all security staff are obliged to display. I mentioned this to Terry and Dave and made a joke that he was probably here illegally and wasn't a licensed security officer. Not thinking too much more about this, I carried on watching the flood of people entering the now packed bar. Dave offered to settle the bar bill and we agreed to move on to somewhere quieter.

While Dave was at the bar, the Russian bouncer came over towards our table. I heard Terry lean over and ask him where his licence was. A look of panic flashed across the man's face, but he composed himself and, in very broken English, replied pretty aggressively, 'What has this got to do with you?'

Terry produced his warrant card. This put more panic in the doorman's face and he swiftly disappeared into the crowd. Terry and I raised our eyebrows at the response but we got up to leave and went over to the bar to join Dave before exiting.

The next thing, all hell broke loose.

As I linked up with Terry just outside the entrance, eight

uniformed police swooped upon us. There were so many coppers you would have though we were gunmen on a rampage. It was like something out of an American SWAT bust. By this time, Dave had come out of the bar and was looking equally bewildered. I could see a special constable getting extremely agitated but then a police van came tearing up with sirens blaring and blue lights flashing. It screeched to a halt just yards from us.

Before we knew what was happening, the special constable and another officer approached Terry, asked him to step to one side and cuffed him. As they bundled him into the back of the van, he turned to me and said, 'Get out of here.' The van sped away at high speed and Dave and I were left standing there, stunned. Dave rang his Detective Inspector, to tell him what had happened to Terry. When he came off the phone, he told me to go home.

'Look, you're a covert source. You need to get out of here,' he said.

'Listen,' I said. 'The only place I'm going is down the nick to sort this out. After all, I'm the only witness for Terry and, if it means blowing my cover to get him out of this mess, then so be it.'

Dave tried to talk me out of it, but I insisted. It seemed clear to me I needed to do something about it. Although our contact had begun on an intelligence basis, we'd worked so closely over the years I'd been spying on Greenpeace that I considered him a mate. He'd had my back over the whole Downing Street situation and I wanted to show him that I wouldn't abandon him now.

Dave established that Terry had been arrested and where he had been taken so we jumped a cab and headed there. My orders were that if I was to stay then under no circumstances should I disclose any of my genuine details and to use my covert cover name Chris Tucker. I should give my address as Police Headquarters.

It seemed absurd to me that the police could arrest a Special Branch officer on next to no evidence of any wrongdoing. It was madness. I knew that if this were to end up in court then I would be in a real catch-22. If I gave evidence on behalf of Terry, I'd blow my cover, but I didn't want to see him go down on some spurious charge. By then, it was 6 p.m. and I had the feeling it was going to be a long night.

In the police station, a sergeant came to speak to us. I left the talking to Dave. We were shown into the station canteen, then almost deserted save for a few coppers in an adjoining TV room. Dave sloped off to make some discreet calls to his superiors but, while he was on the phone, a plainclothes officer approached me and tried to make small talk. I wasn't engaging but eventually he came to the point and asked for a quiet word about what happened.

Incredibly, he actually asked to have an 'off the record' chat – breaking the first rule of the Police and Criminal Evidence Act. It's illegal for that to happen. It has to be a formal witness statement or nothing. Dave then appeared and asked the officer what he thought he was doing. The plainclothes cop sloped off and Dave relayed this bizarre turn of events to his bosses.

We were made to sweat it out until 1 a.m. By then, Special Branch advised me to grant the cops that off-the-record chat after all. They reckoned we had nothing to lose by playing into their hands and it would allow me to remain anonymous.

It was only then we were told that Terry had been arrested

for racially abusing the Russian bouncer. Shocked that so much could have been made out of that brief exchange in the pub, I was even more amazed to learn that the so-called victim hadn't even yet provided a witness statement. Terry had also been further arrested in the custody suite on suspicion of handling a stolen credit card – the one issued to him by Special Branch. The credit card was seized as evidence.

A female CID officer came to take my account but what happened next was bizarre. Carefully placed next to her note pad was the CID officer's radio, which was turned up quite loud and to the point where the radio traffic could be easily heard by everyone both inside the room and outside as well. It struck me as a distraction tactic and one that could be used to explain any discrepancies in my account or her ability to take it down correctly.

As I went through the events of that day, mistakes were constantly made by the CID officer and I spent more time correcting them than concentrating on the content that was needed to correct a very unacceptable situation.

I asked to read through her version of my account. I'm glad I did because as I suspected my remarks had not been accurately recorded. In one example, where I'd said, 'We had consumed a large meal and had occasional drinks with that meal', she'd written, 'We had consumed a large amount of alcohol with the meal.'

I looked across at the officer and said, 'This is not what I said and that sentence is completely wrong and you know that.'

Despite being a relatively short account, I continued to find these 'errors' in almost every other sentence. The end result was something that resembled a short story written by a five-year-old – untidy, with a large amount of crossing out.

At 3 a.m., Dave was informed that the alleged victim could not be traced. He had vanished from his work at the bar and no one knew where he was. This struck me as the behaviour of someone here illegally.

Terry was eventually released on bail pending the police obtaining a formal statement of complaint from the Russian. As we waited outside the police station for him, I couldn't comprehend how a pleasant afternoon had turned into a police officer's worst nightmare.

A very dishevelled Terry emerged, finally, almost numbed by his experience. All he could do was thank me for sticking by him and, for once, he praised me for disobeying his directions to leave the scene at the bar upon his arrest.

The following morning, I was up early and on the phone to one of the Detective Sergeants to find out what was going to happen. The news was not good. Terry was going to be suspended from duty. The only good news was that I was now able to give a full, detailed account of what had happened. I duly submitted the statement but in the days and weeks that followed Terry was taking things very hard indeed and was in despair over the incident.

While, behind the scenes, arguments raged between the police forces, it transpired that the alleged victim could still not be traced. It seemed he had indeed been employed illegally and had breached his visa conditions.

Once the dust had settled, Terry was reinstated in SB and the matter was eventually forgotten. My cover, which had come precariously close to being blown, remained intact – but for how long?

CHAPTER 17

NO IMMUNITY

The constant whirring of the rotor blades was getting louder. Surely, they couldn't spot me.

I tried to make myself smaller, in the hope this would make a difference but suddenly I felt really exposed. For three days I'd felt I was completely enclosed but now it seemed they were looking down directly on top of me. 'Go on, bugger off,' I said under my breath.

Still it kept hovering, though. I was stuck. There was no way I could come out now. I just had to hope this was a routine fly by and I was simply paranoid. Had they seen me? Could I expect the police or security to come roaring up any second? How long would they sit this out? Well, that was one thing I had on them. If a test of endurance was what they were after then I had the upper hand. I could sit this out for as long as I wanted.

I had spent three days already in a hedge. I could wait

some more. That's what it's like when you're in the middle of a CROP (covert rural observation point). Here, in Bridgwater, Somerset, I'd constructed a makeshift hide in the bush and it had been my home. I sat, ate and even did the toilet here. This was hardcore surveillance. My target was Hinkley Point power station and, as all nuclear sites should be, it was well secured.

After what seemed like an eternity, the chopper rose in the sky and slowly moved off. I breathed out again and readjusted my position. I was sure I hadn't been spotted. I'd taken enough precautions after all. To make sure I arrived and departed undetected, I had been arriving here under the hours of darkness, parking my car – a motor I'd hired specifically for this job – discreetly some distance away, and staying here until nightfall meant it was safe to retreat again. Any rubbish I took with me – and that included any body waste I'd passed into plastic bags – so as to leave not a trace that I had ever been here.

So far, I'd been able to spy on the activity at the nuclear power station quite successfully. Greenpeace were planning to hit it at some point with a protest and they needed some pre-op surveillance. My aim was to establish the movement of the nuclear waste, the patrol pattern of the nuclear defence police, identify the strategic points that were manned and, funnily enough, to monitor the presence of the helicopters.

I'd noted the movements of the security, the amount of traffic and, crucially, the movement of any nuclear waste units leaving under escort. Part of my mission, was to establish the systems in place for the transportation of nuclear waste. The contentious issue of nuclear power was once again on the agenda. In 2007, the government would have to make a decision on its long-term energy strategy or face a real threat of the lights going out around 2020 because of a fuel shortage. Ageing nuclear power stations needed to be replaced and there was a call for new reactors to be built to solve the energy crisis, while the technology for renewable sources was still being developed.

Everything was up for grabs and Greenpeace knew, if it didn't act now, and have a say in the debate, they might lose a chance to influence policy at this crucial time.

So, here I was, compiling a timetable of movements and a dossier on security for the action unit to decide if necessary steps were to be taken to propel the safety of these power stations back into the limelight. There was feeling within the organisation that the old fears about the viability of nuclear power had been forgotten. The terror caused by disasters like Chernobyl had been replaced by complacency that really this controversial form of energy could in fact be the answer to the country's problems.

The subject was one close to Steve's heart. He had a history with nuclear power stations, having twice broken into Sizewell B, in Suffolk – once, to oppose nuclear power and, once, to show how vulnerable it was to terrorist attack. He was found guilty of criminal damage on each occasion and narrowly escaped community service or even jail. He wouldn't think twice of tackling this place if it deserved it.

I'd felt quite honoured that he'd entrusted me with this one. It was a sign of the trust he had in me. I relished the opportunity to be out, working on my own, developing my own strategy. I should have been doing this work ages ago like I knew I should have been. I always worked solo on covert jobs as I trust myself more and know that if it goes wrong it's my mistake, and it's up to me to get out of it by thinking quickly on my feet.

I'd spent some time scoping out the best vantage point. I'd checked into a B&B – a converted old farmhouse reasonably close by – under the pretext that I was birdwatcher. It was a good ruse and allowed me to be seen with binoculars, to come and go at unsociable hours and to wander the hedgerows. It allowed me to appear to be scanning the skies when actually I was marking the security cameras and monitoring their movement.

The only trouble was that it was early winter and absolutely freezing. Not the best climate to be stuck in a bush from an hour before dawn to an hour after dusk. It brought back memories of Northern Ireland, where often we would have to maintain a CROP position for three weeks at a time. It's standard military procedure, to be holed up, making notes, taking photographs and monitoring a situation.

I would return to my farmhouse B&B to questions like, 'Did you have a nice day birdwatching?' Or, 'Spot anything interesting today?'

I'd spin some waffle about an elusive lesser-spotted warbler I was trying to find and leave it at that.

The day following the helicopter scare, I was back in my bush when my phone started to vibrate. It was Terry.

'Where are you?' he said.

'I can't tell you that,' I whispered, even though I knew there was probably no one for about half a mile.

'You're not in Somerset are you?'

I didn't answer.

'Not sniffing about a nuclear power station?' he said.

I coughed.

'It's just they've pinged a car hired in your name. I just want to check it's actually you that's using it.'

'Yeah, it's me,' I said, cursing my luck.

'That's OK, I thought as much. I'll just let them know there's no need to panic. We've got it in hand. You're not going to storm the place are you?

'No,' I said. 'Just pre-op detail.'

'Good-oh,' he said. 'Cheerio.'

It could have been worse, I suppose. If I'd have been any other Greenpeace activist, I would've been burned and possibly busted. At least I could continue my surveillance and report back to Greenpeace, with them none the wiser. In any event, I was freezing my bollocks off and there's only so much of sitting in a bush a man can stomach. I would happily have continued had the job merited it but was also relieved of the chance to knock it on the head.

I relayed the information I'd gathered to Steve – and to SB. Steve was delighted and impressed that I'd done such a thorough job. It could be put into good use in the future, he said, but for the time being they were working on something more pressing. They were planning another coal run.

It was several weeks before I got the exact details but, once again, I was heartened that they wanted me involved. Harry Taylor was the man calling the shots on it, which amazed me, but I towed the line and appeared as keen as mustard to be included. I wondered what the target would be. It was now a year and a half on from the Downing Street stunt and, although it was successful, to hit it again might have appeared lame. Carbon emissions were still a hot topic but I couldn't think of an alternative target. I'm sure Greenpeace had a clever idea.

Harry called the drivers in for a briefing session in Islington.

'Right,' he said, 'as you're aware, we're planning another major protest against a prominent target. I can now tell you the target will once again be 10 Downing Street.'

To my astonishment, a couple of the activists got quite excited about this. They must be easily pleased, I thought.

Taylor went on: 'We'll be sending a message to Tony Blair that his failure to act on climate change is unacceptable. The protest will be timed to coincide with the publication of a report from the world's leading authority on climate change saying that global warming is significantly worse than first feared and there is now irrefutable evidence that it is a man-made problem.'

The operation was codenamed 'Project Heap'. There would be two trucks this time, Taylor informed us. Possibly eager to avoid the same mistake as last time, when the HGV was too big for Central London, he said this job would be smaller in scale but, hopefully, no less effective. The plan was to travel to the Farm and practice the roles we had. There would be two trucks, mine and one other laden with the coal. We would drive to a rendezvous on the South Bank in London, meet with a minibus full of volunteers, and head straight to Downing Street and dump 15 tonnes of coal at Tony's front door again. The Greenpeace side of things was clear, but the problems came from a different angle, the police.

I flashed the intelligence over to SB. This time I felt more relaxed and in a strong position. We knew the target now, the date and the time. In some ways I didn't need to be involved. Yet, here I was, going to be driving the truck. It was a detail that was to prove hugely problematic.

A meeting was hastily arranged with SB and the normal routine of anti-surveillance and signing of the immunity forms took place. It should have been a clearer process because we knew the target this time but if anything this set of circumstances made me nervous.

'What if they change the location?' I said.

'To where?' Steve asked.

'I don't know, but there were problems with their plans last time. What's to say they won't fuck it up this time too?'

'We can't predict that,' Steve said.

'No, but we can cover my back in case they do. My immunity only covers Downing Street, doesn't it? Am I covered if they have a last minute change of mind and go somewhere else?'

'No,' said Steve.

'What if they dump it a few yards away in Horse Guards?' I asked.

'Technically, no,' Steve said. 'You're only covered for the specific location.'

'So,' I said, starting to get exasperated. 'Can't we factor in any other potential targets like last time?'

'But we know the target.'

'Yes,' I said, 'but I'm screwed if it deviates from that. It's what I'm trying to say.'

Steve looked at me quite calmly. 'Well then,' he said, 'you'll just have to find away of extracting yourself before it gets to that stage.'

'I'm driving a bloody truck.'

'All the more reason to make sure you're not on it when the coal is dumped then,' said Steve.

'Don't let it get to the arrest stage,' I said mocking the earlier advice I'd received from SB. 'I remember.'

'Good job you do,' said Terry. 'Last time, they let these do-gooders get on with it. And because you were there it was problematic for them to arrest everyone. This time, the chances are they won't be so lenient. You've got your immunity. Think yourself lucky. If they switch the targets you need to get out of there or you could find yourself getting nicked. It's a different ballgame this time round.'

'Thanks for the reassurance,' I said. I left shaking my head.

For some reason, I had a bad feeling about this job. The Met, in being very restrictive over what my immunity would cover, was tying my hands this time. Potentially they were risking five years of deep infiltration on my part, simply due to the rigid constraints of the senior upper echelons of the Yard. Hadn't they been pleased with the work I'd done on the last Downing Street stunt? Were their memories that short? Just one stupid unconsidered call would wreck my hard work and place me in a difficult situation operationally. I needed flexibility and I needed the Met to be more relaxed and understanding of my position on the ground. I was the one at the sharp end, and I felt, as normal, the desk jockeys had no idea of the impact of their decisions.

I had a real problem if the plans changed in the slightest as I would be open to prosecution. This would include a change from Downing Street to the Foreign Office next door, just a matter of yards away, but I would not be covered. But, as Terry had confirmed, the Met just would not give way. Of course the operation could go as planned but I was beginning to fear that, when it came down to it, they employed the American system of 'use, abuse and burn'.

I arrived at the Farm mid-afternoon and we began practising our drills and timings. There was a problem with my tipping mechanism; although the hydraulics were engaging on the tipper lift, it was taking more than five seconds to kick in, and this was to be a vital time and could mean the difference between getting it dumped and getting caught and stopped. I reported it to the guys at the Farm but it was ignored. After this we headed out and fuelled up. Another problem was that my fuel cap was jammed on so I could not take on diesel, and again the decision was taken to risk it.

From my conversations with the other crew, it seemed things were open to change. Downing Street might not be the target after all. At that stage, no alternative was being suggested but it only served to ratchet up my apprehension.

I had one last go at impressing upon Terry the importance of extending my immunity but it was falling on deaf ears. The Met was just not listening to the guys on the ground, the ones who had to go through all of this. I'd always believed that the most important person to listen to was the agent, but it saddens me to say the Met thought otherwise. I feared it was playing a reckless game.

It was with a heavy heart that I resumed my duties and joined the other lads preparing the trucks for the following day's mission. As before we plastered the sides with Greenpeace logos and then covered them up to avoid detection until the last minute. Next we sheeted over all the coal. It was midnight when we finally finished.

When we were all done, we moved to a B&B in Sawbridgeworth for some much needed food, a couple of beers and, finally, bed. We would only have time for a few hours kip, as before, but I suffered a restless night. I still could not confirm the target 100 per cent, as in my mind there were too many factors going wrong. I managed to get a final message out to SB that the rendezvous was still on the South Bank, regardless of where the ultimate destination would be. I reminded them the target might be changeable. I had to pray that common sense might prevail. Surely, they would pass this information on to the Met. A covert surveillance team could shadow us from there and it would mean they would be able to follow things as they progressed. It seemed more sensible than leaving it all to me. Once I left the B&B, it would be practically impossible for me to get any more messages out, while I was surrounded by the other crew.

I couldn't shake the feeling that something bad was going to happen. I felt in some ways I was both the problem and the solution and suddenly I wasn't confident of the role I was performing for either Greenpeace or SB. By supplying all the details to SB, I was jeopardising the entire stunt for Greenpeace. The Met had let them get on with it on the last occasion but this time they might choose to thwart it and earn some cheap brownie points for themselves in the process. A higher than normal police presence might scare off Harry Taylor. Alternatively, he might choose to dump at an alternative location. Then I could find myself completely compromised – my cover blown. Fuck. What do I do?

I carried out my own risk assessment. I couldn't back out now. Walking away would blow me out of the water as far as Greenpeace were concerned. I couldn't also take part in any stunt. That would be crossing the line. My only option was to frustrate the entire task. If I somehow stopped the job going ahead it was better than it happening at all. If I managed to do it cleverly enough, I might live to spy another day. I was just so frustrated with the Met. The powers-that-be didn't deserve to have someone this diligent thinking of every eventuality for them. I should leave them to get on with it but I knew I wouldn't be able to live with myself – and any event I couldn't risk a prosecution.

All manner of thoughts went through my head. Could I engineer it so the trucks broke down? Could I scupper things by taking the wrong route? Would feigning illness at the wheel have the desired effect? What if the truck was in an accident?

I had to think quickly.

There was a knock on my bedroom door. It was 3.45 am. It was time to go to work.

CHAPTER 18

COVER BLOWN

At 4 a.m., six Greenpeace protestors and me were standing freezing our socks off at the back of the B&B waiting to be ferried back to the Farm. There wasn't much chatter from anyone in the short journey through the country roads to Greenpeace's now not so secret location.

Half an hour later, the final checks made to the lorries, we were ready to go. Brian, one of the other drivers, was going to be taking the lead truck. I was driving the second one, on my own. This was a bit of luck. It could mean that, should there be a change of plan, I might be able to get a message to SB after all. Kevin was in a guide vehicle with other members of the crew.

We were ready to depart and slowly we edged our way out of the Farm and towards the M11. Just before the junction with the M25, I began my plan of disruption. I called ahead to the other truck and the guide vehicle and reported that, as a tail end Charlie and someone very experienced in surveillance, I had detected a possible tail behind us since we had joined the M11.

The message was flashed over to Harry Taylor, who was going to be coordinating things on the ground in London. His word back was just to carry on as normal. I hadn't expected any other response but I hoped some elements of doubt might creep into his thinking.

We snaked our way through Waltham Forest and into Hackney Marshes, where Brian, driving the truck that had a heating problem just days before, signalled that he needed to stop as the engine was overheating again. Maybe my luck was in after all. There was a good chance these rickety old rust buckets would never make it to Downing Street. Even a short stop would mean we would miss our deadline for the rendezvous point. That would please Taylor no end. Sure enough, Harry was already getting agitated and was calling Kevin in the guide car telling him to speed things up.

We sat idle for half an hour, while Brian took some water on, and then, eventually, we moved off towards the Angel, not far from the Greenpeace office. Brian was having real difficulties in his truck and had failed to keep up with the guide car. We were now both well off the planned route by now. This was going better than planned. For all my worrying during the night about how to engineer a mishap, fate was playing its own hand in the proceedings. Kevin was eventually contacted, told of the break in the convoy, but the message relayed back to us was that, simply, we were to get to the rendezvous as best we could and as quickly as we could.

Just as we were driving near the back of City Road, we were struck with more good fortune – depending on how you looked at it. Brian was forced to pull over once again. The brake fluid was now boiling over, rendering the truck dangerous to drive. Kevin, in the guide car, was called and we all met up in the street where the lead truck had broken down.

Several heated phone calls were exchanged between Kevin and Harry, while I relaxed in my cab. This was getting better by the minute. Then I came up with an idea that might improve things for me yet further. I got out and approached a clearly stressed out Kevin.

'Look, this truck is knackered. The best thing to do would be to take it back to HQ and out of the way. It's dangerous to drive it in its current state so why don't I take it back and Brian can continue in my truck?'

Kevin looked at me quizzically.

'I'm the most experienced driver here,' I went on. 'I'm a police class-one advanced driver, with a lot of experience driving vehicles. If anyone else drove it and had an accident, Greenpeace would be in serious bother. I'm the best person for the job.'

My intention was to extract myself from the job without suspicion. In reality, I wouldn't take the truck anywhere but would sit and wait for the breakdown people. Kevin seemed to agree with my forceful, out-of-concern-for-them approach, but wanted to run it by Harry. He had other ideas.

'No,' he told Kevin, 'get Ross to carry on as normal with his truck.'

Even worse, he told Kevin to get Trevor, a regular

Greenpeace staffer and a close contact of Harry Taylor's who had been riding with Brian in his cab, to jump in with me. Shit. Now I'd have no chance to relaying any messages to Terry at SB.

By now, we were 90 minutes behind schedule and, with it now being rush hour, the traffic was bad. I really did have to think hard and carefully. Just a moment ago, it had all been looking quite rosy, but now I was in a sticky situation. Pushing through the morning traffic I drove deliberately slowly. I wanted to give the Met every chance to pick us up by patrols or helicopter. There was no evidence of that happening any time soon, however, at that stage, with the covers still on and the Greenpeace signs obscured it wasn't obvious what our intentions were. My best hope was that the Met was keeping an eye on the rendezvous.

Eventually, we arrived at Upper Ground, on the South Bank, the meeting point, where we met with about a dozen volunteer foot soldiers that had arrived in a minibus. We stripped the covers off the truck, exposing the massive Greenpeace signs along the length on both sides. My crewmate, Trevor, seemed intent on sticking to me like glue. Even when I went to take a leak he stayed practically on my shoulder!

Harry was then on the phone, panicking. He was on Westminster Bridge and he said the place was teaming with cops. What the hell were the Met playing at? I'd been assured there would have been a normal presence around Downing Street. Was their plan to stop the trucks as they passed over the bridge? If so, that would have knackered my immunity.

The sight of so many police had unnerved Taylor. It must have served to confirm something he'd been itching to do all along because, almost immediately, he ordered a change of plan.

'Scrap Number 10,' he yelled at Kevin. 'We're switching to DEFRA in Smith Square.'

Fuck. I knew this would happen. DEFRA, the Department of Environment, Food and Rural Affairs, was actually an obvious target, I had to give him that, and it was close by. Smith Square was on the other side of Parliament Square from Downing Street and from the south side would be easiest accessed via Lambeth Bridge.

From my point of view, it was a disaster, however. It was the last thing I wanted to happen. DEFRA meant no immunity. If I were in any way involved when the cops showed up, I'd be arrested, with little chance of being sorted after the event. And, given what Terry had told me, the police this time were keen to crack some skulls and nick the protesters.

The order to mount up and go came and still I could not see any surveillance nearby. Things were desperate, as the police knew days before where the rendezvous was but had not acted. By luck, Kevin did not know the way to Smith Square. I saw a chance to buy myself some time so I told him I did and that I thought it was best to go the long way round to avoid any police attention.

We slowly drove from Upper Ground, along Blackfriars Road towards Waterloo. My hope was that a police uniform patrol would be around and would stop us before we could get anywhere near our new objective. There was no chance of me being able to get a message to SB to alert them to the change of plan.

South London was my old manor. I knew it like the back

of my hand so I led Kevin on a merry dance in the hope that some eagle-eyed cop would spot the Greenpeace sign and call a halt to this little operation, in the same way that the traffic officer had scuppered the HGV at Downing Street. I steered them down towards Battersea Bridge, past the power station. As luck would have it, India 99, the police helicopter, was just taking off from the nearby helipad. This is it, I thought. Only a matter of time before it spies the huge coal truck and alerts the cops on the ground.

We trundled over the bridge and turned right to head along the Embankment. The helicopter sailed high into the sky and out over north London. This was hopeless. I had to come up with some other way of screwing the operation. I thought about breaking sharply to cause someone to crash into the back of me. The trouble was I didn't know what the result of any collision would be. One might certainly abort the mission but what if someone got hurt. How could I live with myself? I couldn't trade public safety for stopping the stunt. You have no choice, I told myself, you'll just have to go through with this.

As we approached the MI5 building, I saw on my left-hand side two armed officers on patrol walking toward us. I slowed down, as if inviting them to stop us, but to my sheer amazement they just kept chatting to each other and took no notice of the heavily signed vehicle that was almost at a stop right beside them. I cursed heavily under my breath for their stupidity and lack of observation skills.

I slowly moved forward to the north side of Lambeth Bridge and saw coming onto the roundabout a double-crewed police van. This was my chance, I thought. I should have given way to the van from my right but, on this occasion, I pushed ahead to get onto the roundabout and deliberately stalled the engine right in front of them. This is it. I waited for the doors to open and the coppers to jump out. Instead, they just waited patiently until I restarted the engine and moved forward. Once again, I couldn't believe it. The mighty Greenpeace sign had been staring them in the face. What was it with the police today? How could this be? What were they waiting for, an invitation? It was a gift to them!

I was now on to Plan Z – to do nothing at the scene. I approached the junction with Smith Square and saw Harry Taylor rush into the road and start frantically pointing left into the square. I turned left and went to the far corner where the guide car had branched off and left us alone. I started to come back round the square again to get a fix on my target when Taylor appeared in the centre of the square.

'Get a fucking move on!' he shouted. 'What the bloody hell are you doing?'

By now, I was pissed off with both the Met and Taylor. As I came round to the entrance of the DEFRA offices, there was a black taxi cab sitting outside, right where I needed to be. Once again, luck was on my side. I had no option but to wait for the cab to move.

'Look what you've done,' he said, as if the presence of the cab was my fault. He ran to the taxi driver to get him to move while I sat in the middle of the road waiting patiently for a space to appear.

I said to Trevor, in the cab with me, that he should man the tipper while I got out to make sure the back lifted up properly.

He looked at me blankly. I was going against my orders,

which had been to stay in the cab, with the windows up and the doors locked to prevent any police trying to stop us in the act, and work the tipper from there.

'Remember, there's a time delay,' I said to Kevin. 'And with these ropey hydraulics I better kick the swing flap at the back to empty the coal.'

Meanwhile, Taylor was having little joy convincing the cabbie to move out the way. Clearly the taxi driver didn't warm to Taylor. He locked his doors and refused to budge. This operation was turning into a complete disaster. Its codename should have been changed to 'Project Heap of Shit'.

Eventually, however, the fare arrived, got in and the taxi drove off. I roared into position, reversed up, and jumped out, shouting at my crewmate to hit the tipper controls. I was busying myself with the release of the flap when Taylor ran over.

'Why are you not in the cab?' he demanded. 'Why is the tip not lifting?'

'Trevor's doing it. The mechanism's not working well enough. I'm here to make sure it works,' I said.

'I told you to do it,' he shouted.

Suddenly, he pushed me back. In a flash he was gone though, jumping into the cab and increased the power on the hydraulics. The back of the truck elevated and three and a half tonnes of coal shed its load onto the pavement right outside the doors of DEFRA.

It was only then that I realised that Trevor, the crewmate who'd stuck to me like glue since I'd taken over the duties of driving the one and only truck, had disappeared. I briefly saw him and Taylor speaking to each other but then he'd scarpered. I was now suspicious that this guy had been a Greenpeace plant all along – or certainly someone put in place by Taylor. Had he felt he needed someone to watch over me?

The rest of the volunteers helped get the remainder of the coal out of the lorry. Then there was a strange few moments when nothing happened. There was no commotion, no onrushing cops arresting everyone. It took 20 minutes for any police to show and, when they did, it was two motorcycle cops. I spoke to one of the traffic officers. He was perfectly calm but was keen for me to move the truck. Then a CO11 public order intelligence unit arrived. The motorcyclists disappeared. I heard one of the CO11 officers (basically, a unit from the Commissioner's Office in Scotland Yard) requesting backup from the Territorial Support Group (TSG), the riot cops, my old unit. 'Demonstration has got out of hand,' I heard him saying, 'requesting assistance.' It was all going pear-shaped now.

The TSG must have been on stand-by because they were there in no time. Now it looked certain we were going to be detained. The words of SB came back into my mind. 'Don't let it get to the arrest stage.' Great advice in an ideal world but in reality it's not always easy to implement.

I saw a chance though to influence my own fate. I had taken my police issue gloves with me, primarily because it was biting cold, but now I saw a chance to perhaps put them to good use. They are distinctive gloves, which only police use. I put them on as I spoke to the CO11 officer.

'All is not what it appears to be here,' I said.

'What do you mean?' he said.

I stroked my chin with my gloves, not too subtly.

'You need to speak with your guv'nor,' I said.

'What?' he looked even more confused now.

'Look,' I said, extending my hand. Finally, the penny dropped.

'Oh,' he said. 'Right, I see.'

Just then another police officer who had turned up and was on the other side of the road looked at me and said, very loudly: 'I know him. He was on the DPG.'

I froze. I couldn't believe it. What the fuck was he playing at? Now this was going really tits-up. I had no idea who within Greenpeace had heard him say that he knew me from the Diplomatic Protection Group. It was a colossal fuck-up. For all he knew, I could have been an undercover cop on a covert op. It was like sticking a luminous arrow above my head.

I didn't have anything to lose now. 'Contact SB,' I said to the friendly CO11 officer. 'Ask your guv'nor before you decide to do anything.'

'Ok, then, hold on,' he said. He then spoke to a female inspector who had arrived on the scene from Belgravia. As this was going on, other officers took our details. We were all lined up and videoed. It was explained to me that I was likely to be arrested for public order offences. I had to hope sanity would prevail with the CO11 officer.

Meanwhile, the excitable PC who had done his best to blow my cover was taken to one side.

The CO11 cop came back. To me, he said, 'We're going to report you, no arrest. You're free to go.'

That was good enough for me. I didn't hang about to be told twice. I jumped into the lorry and, taking some of the volunteers with me, drove back to Islington. Just, as at 4 a.m.

that morning, there was little chat in the cab on the way back. The contrast with Downing Street was palpable. Then you could sense the elation of a job well done. Here, everyone was flat. They knew it had been a hollow victory.

For my part, I just wanted to get the hell out of there. What with Taylor's reaction, Trevor's spying on me and the unbelievable lack of discretion from the police officer, I felt sure my cover was blown within Greenpeace. I felt a deep sense of frustration. Fucking amateurs, the lot of them. No one seemed to care that I'd put five years of my life into this. I'd supplied intelligence they could only dream of and I thought our relationship was working well. Today had just proved to me that when it suits them they would cut you loose.

Back at the Greenpeace HQ, I dumped the truck. Harry Taylor wasn't back yet, so I collared Gemma. She looked at me with a strangely detached look on her face that only confirmed it was the end of the road for me as far as Greenpeace UK were concerned.

I found my car that had been sitting there since before the operation began and drove home before Taylor and his stooges got back.

Clear of the office, I rang Terry and filled him in what happened. He seemed genuinely remorseful about how it had turned out.

'And you won't believe what else happened,' I said. 'One uniformed cop shouted out across the square that he recognised me from DPG.'

'You're fucking joking,' Terry said. 'That won't be allowed to lie.'

'Well, I saw him being taken to one side. I don't know if that means he'll get a talking to.'

'We'll make sure he does,' Terry said.

A week later Terry got back in touch. The fall-out from DEFRA continued.

'We got it in the neck from the Yard,' he said. 'And we did get a bollocking from the DI [Detective Inspector] for your insinuation that you were on a covert op. What was that all about?' Terry said.

'I was only doing what you guys told me. Don't let it get to the arrest stage. Remember? I did what I had to do without showing out.'

'We didn't mean impersonate an undercover cop,' said Terry. 'That didn't go down well at all.'

'The CO11 officer just assumed I was a serving officer and I didn't make him think otherwise. I let him draw his own conclusions,' I said.

'Well, whatever, you'll be getting your knuckles rapped from the DI over that.'

Terry did tell me that the officer who'd blurted out that he recognised me was dealt with accordingly.

'He was summoned for a chat with inspector,' Terry explained. 'And told in no uncertain terms that what he saw that day he did not see, what he heard he did not hear. If he repeats it to anyone disciplinary action will follow. I hear he got the message.'

In the days that followed, I received a warning letter from the DCI (Detective Chief Inspector) at CO11. It said that I participated in an unauthorised demo and that I'd been reported for 'causing an obstruction by depositing a quantity of coal on the highway under section 148 Highways Act 1980'.

It said I'd face no further action but added that the local

authority may well bill Greenpeace for the cost of removing the coal.

I also received a letter from someone in Greenpeace's activist and logistics support team, detailing what to do should charges arise from the DEFRA stunt, emphasising that Greenpeace lawyers would provide representation and the organisation would meet any costs. I knew it wouldn't be relevant to but I'm sure for the other activists it was reassuring to receive such a supportive correspondence. It was obvious, however, that word from the action team hadn't filtered upstairs to where the logistics team were situated, otherwise I doubt I would have been included in the mail out.

As it was, that letter was the last correspondence I ever had with Greenpeace UK. Since then, Greenpeace UK have never used my services again, and I was effectively an outcast, although they have never said this.

I blamed the Met for compromising my position. It wasn't through any slip-up in my behaviour. If only I had been given the correct authority, there would have been no suspicion to this day.

Even though I'd carried out a lot of tasks for them and earned praise for my help with the Downing Street job, my reluctance to fully participate in Project Heap must have raised suspicions, especially in Taylor. Even though they would never have been able to prove I was a double agent, there was enough evidence to suggest they would be better dispensing with my services. It had been a good run, lucrative at times and challenging nearly always.

My time as an eco-warrior, however, was at an end.

EPILOGUE

It was a cold and otherwise uneventful day in Kiev when I first got word that something had gone seriously wrong with a high-profile undercover operation back in the UK.

The case involved a police covert operator by the name of Mark Kennedy. The news coming through was fragmented and sketchy in places, so was hard to actually piece together the events that were unfolding. However, the grapevine was working overtime and the word was slowly but surely filtering through from the intelligence community that something major had happened.

I was in Ukraine completing a risk assessment survey for a client but on hearing those first snippets to do with the case I couldn't concentrate on the task at hand. This was too close to home. An undercover agent caught infiltrating an environmental group? I had to find out more.

It emerged that Kennedy – who was using the aliases Mark Stone and 'Flash' – had infiltrated several green groups between 2003 and 2010, while attached to the police service's National Public Order Intelligence Unit (NPOIU), before he was unmasked by political activists as an undercover policeman. His covert role came to light when the case against six activists accused of conspiracy to commit aggravated trespass at Ratcliffe-on-Soar Power Station, in Nottinghamshire, collapsed after Kennedy's activities as an undercover policeman were revealed.

Surprisingly, my understanding was that the first real indication that something was amiss came from within Greenpeace, which, as we know now, had a few activists freelancing with another green group who were directly involved in the Ratcliffe-On-Soar Power Station protest. Initial incoming reports suggested that the green group had concerns over Kennedy and his status after claims aired by a female activist close to the man himself. There were suspicions he was an undercover cop sent to spy on a number of green groups.

But before any of the revelations became public, there was frenzied activity on the part of the activists about how to play it. Some were cautious not to call Kennedy in without good cause. Yet others felt if it was true that he was a covert officer then he had to be outed quickly. Charges were still pending against activists who'd taken part in a protest at the power station. If Kennedy was a cop, some felt his existence could muddy the waters substantially enough to affect any subsequent court case.

Many hours were spent deliberating over what to do and, from what I hear from my sources, it was at this point that Kennedy really had began to fear that he was about to be exposed.

I can only feel for what he must have been going through at that time. The Metropolitan officer was more embedded than I ever was and, because of his role within the police, had much more to lose, but I sympathised with his plight. I knew only too well what it was like to be a double agent and I knew how bitter his betrayal would be felt among the groups he'd infiltrated. In the fall-out that followed, he claimed he had been under extreme provocation and was left high and dry by his handlers when he tried to raise his concerns.

Yet, as I investigated his case, I began to ask the question: where did the fault lie? He knew his cover had been blown. He just didn't know how it would be handled. In fact, I was told the feeling inside the green groups was not to expose him. It was felt that by doing so would undermine the work of environmentalists and disrupt future action by any group including Greenpeace itself. This debate went on for a long time and, internally at least, exposed wide divisions in the green movement.

It also seemed that some activists were rebutting any beliefs that Kennedy was a cop, but the fire was lit only for it to develop into a blaze some days later. The whole episode – which came to light in January 2010 – was unsavoury and called into question the whole ethics behind covert operations and the role performed by undercover cops. Could Kennedy have extricated himself earlier without blowing his cover?

Kennedy claims he made repeated requests to his superiors explaining his predicament but it either fell on deaf ears or he was encouraged to simply carry on.

So, did Kennedy get in too deep? Did he lose sight of his objectives? These were the questions his handlers would have been asking. They all point to the burning issue: did he become an agent provocateur? Such a conclusion could be sustainable if Kennedy had shown a willingness to over extend himself and to facilitate actions that were in essence criminal acts.

There is a very fine line between a covert operator and an agent provocateur and that line can often be blurry. It was a situation I always had to be aware of and was continually assessing. When I took part in the Downing Street coal dump, people could argue that I crossed that line. In my view, though, I balanced my involvement always with the information I was passing on to the authorities and I always took their lead on how far I could push it.

When I stopped short of pulling the lever to dump the coal in Smith Square, I was demonstrating that I was playing no part in the demo.

Kennedy's case will have repercussions for the way police carry out long-term investigations. He felt he had to act in a certain way or his cover would be blown.

The ramifications of the Kennedy affair have without doubt sent massive shock waves through not only the police Covert Operations Branch but also the entire legal system and ACPO (Association of Chief Police Officers). The case will haunt operations for a very long time with any future cases being defended robustly whilst citing the Kennedy case and all its components.

This naturally brought into question many of the operating procedures and policies that exist and emanate from ACPO guidelines. There is no doubt that there always has been a degree of 'flexibility' of the rules at local level and it is this interpretation that has in some instances wrongly eroded away the integrity of covert policing here in the UK.

In fairness to the Met, this scenario is not one you can plan and account for. As a very wise sergeant once told me during my early years as a cop, 'Where there are humans there are fuck-ups.'

No amount of psychological profiling can eliminate the unexpected purely because it is impossible to know how an undercover officer will react until he or she gets on the ground.

They have to be strong psychologically to resist the temptation that always comes your way on covert ops. It doesn't matter what high-level crime you are investigating, whether it be drugs, arms, counterfeit goods or human trafficking, there will be temptations along the way. It could be a lucrative financial reward, women or drugs.

In my time as a covert operator, I have been offered drugs, sex and money. During my five years with Greenpeace, I believe I had eight opportunities to conduct extra-marital affairs that might have led to a greater involvement within the organisation. At the time, the offers can seem very flattering and tempting indeed but, by succumbing, you are open to compromise and jeopardising the entire operation.

By taking backhanders or helping yourself to some of the uncut powder you are trafficking in order to expose a Mr Big, you are inviting criticism that you are little better than the criminals you are meant to be exposing.

The Kennedy case has also shown the spotlight on the units that instigate these operations. Apart from the covert unit, there are two others that gather intelligence by covert methods – the NPOIU (National Public Order Intelligence Unit), which he was attached to, and the CIU (Confidential Intelligence Unit) – which also focus on extremist groups.

The NPOIU performs an intelligence function in relation to politically motivated disorder from illegitimate protests. Until the Kennedy affair, little was known about this secret police unit.

Andrew Gilligan, a journalist from the *Evening Standard*, described it as a 'secretive, Scotland Yard-based police taskforce' whose 'role in controlling dissent is central'. The actual unit was formed on the directions of ACPO in March 1999 and is made up of seconded officers from all over the UK. It is based at a location known for its secrecy – Tintagel House on London's Embankment.

Although seemingly a low-profile unit with a secret background, it is very potent and has a very high degree of influence in decision-making before, during and after covert operations. I was surprised to find the unit was taking an interest in my dealings with Greenpeace. In most of my operational meetings its officers were either there or on the fringes. On one occasion, I was at odds with it over the practicalities of an operation that was taking place. Although not a designated covert ops unit in the real sense of the word it often got involved in such projects and was not overly loved by other police units.

The CIU is concerned with reducing or removing the threat of criminality and or public disorder that arises from domestic extremism.

Whether deliberate or otherwise, domestic extremism is not defined as such for the purpose of the CIU's remit but is loosely categorised as animal rights extremism, environmental extremism, left and right wing extremists and emerging threats.

The unit prides itself on the use of CHIS (covert human intelligence sources), i.e. informants.

The concern with a unit like this is that because it's remit is so widely defined it can extend to take in almost any interest group.

As Henry Porter of the *Guardian* wrote: 'It is evident that the CIU will not be troubled by any public accountability and that the individual who becomes its head will be able to make decisions unilaterally about the nation's politics. If all environmental groups are to be branded extreme, if those who demonstrate against the invasion of Gaza are, as a matter of course, to be regarded as a criminal threat, we will enter a period of enormous tension between the authorities and those people who wish to exercise their legitimate right to demonstrate.'

The CIU first began its recruitment in November 2008, although its existence was acknowledged in February of that year and its critics saw it as a revival of the kind of political policing carried out by MI5 and police Special Branches in the 1970s.

The clandestine role that Mark Kennedy took on for seven years was very comparable to my own within Greenpeace, and the challenges he faced equalled my own over a similar period of time. From all the information I have seen in relation to Kennedy's assignment, there were no difficulties that could not have been overcome. Admittedly, seven years is a long time to be embedded but I know it is possible to function as an undercover officer in those circumstances without your cover being blown.

In my situation, other than the high-ranking officers from New Scotland Yard who failed to acknowledge a switch in targets at the last moment during the Smith Square operation, I cannot fault the conduct of any of the controlling officers. At each stage, I was given options to pull back, pull out or completely terminate an assignment without any recourse to myself. Also, I had available the ear of my immediate controller 24/7 pre-, during and post-operation, and welfare was certainly shown to me as being a priority and consideration. Therefore, it is hard for me to understand that the same opportunities and considerations would not have been afforded to Kennedy during his time in the role.

Perhaps, in the fall-out from this case, more attention needs to be given to the treatment of undercover officers. A thorough overhaul of operating practices and procedures have no doubt already taken place in the wake of such a destructive set-back which most likely ranks as one of the most damaging operations in the history of covert policing. Maybe more research is needed into the emotional pressures infiltrators are under.

It would be instructive to carry out a study of Stockholm syndrome – the phenomenon whereby hostages feel an emotional attachment to their captors – and see if any lessons can be applied to long-term undercover investigators.

The more we understand about the psychological effects at work the better we might be able to train future undercover agents to reduce the chances of this happening again.

It remains to be seen what effect the Kennedy case and my own involvement will have on the green movement. Environmental organisations have been fast in protecting